Studio City

Professional Session Recording for Guitarists

by Carl Verheyen

ISBN 1-57560-341-1
Copyright © 2001 Cherry Lane Music Company
International Copyright Secured
All Rights Reserved

Visit our website at www.cherrylane.com

Contents

Acknowledgments

For Ginny (Virginia Young Hilgren)

I would like to thank the following people for their help in this project:
Jon Chappell at Cherry Lane; Rick Gould at In Concert Photography; Pat Colgan;
Stan Lamendola, Andy Brauer, and all the lads at Andy Brauer Cartage; my band:
bassist Cliff Hugo and drummer Steve DiStanislao; Norik Renson and Brett
Sandberg at Renson Guitar; Brian Banks and Amy Lyngos at Ear to Ear Studios;
and all of the composers, producers, and artists who consented to have their music
and their stories reproduced in this book.

Introduction

Good Morning! It's 8:45 a.m. and you're on the 101 Freeway into Hollywood, running late for that 9:00 a.m. start at Capitol. As you weave in and out of the millions of other commuters, you're thinking: "Shoulda changed those strings on my Rickenbacker 12, they mentioned a Byrds sound . . . do I have any spare 9-volt batteries . . . the tuner is going south . . . I hope I can sneak a parking place on the lot . . . did I call cartage regarding my 2:00 p.m. downbeat at Ocean Way Studios?"

Welcome to the fast lane—the hectic, high-speed world of a studio musician in Los Angeles, California. And welcome to the pages of *Studio City*, the complete collection of columns of the same name that appeared in *Guitar Magazine* from May 1996 to October 1999.

For each installment I wrote about a particular recording session, describing the gear used and the skills required to do the gig. As a whole, these columns provide a broad perspective on a life in music. But it is my sincere hope that individually each column can serve as a mini guitar lesson and provide you with something you can take away and practice.

Roots

I started playing guitar on my 11th birthday. My grandmother gave me a $30 guitar and a year of lessons at $2.50 a week. I was addicted to the guitar early on and my parents had to beg me to stop practicing. I never had a day job, except when I became a box boy one summer to pay off my new Les Paul. Throughout my teens I played in rock 'n' roll bands at the high school dances. During college I had a five-nights-a-week club gig singing with my acoustic guitar. That gig, along with college, ended early when I went on the road. Then there were a few years of sideman work in pickup bands for weddings and parties.

Consequently, by the time I hit age 25, I just sort of fell into studio work as a continuation of making a living playing music. I never set out to be a studio musician; in fact I wasn't really aware the job existed when I was coming up. And as the years progressed, I went from one session a month, to one session a week, to two or three a week, to two or three a day.

Growth

But as this book will subtly reveal, I don't consider studio work alone to be an artistically satisfying end in itself for me. Although many of my peers are content to "punch the clock" and operate within the daily ongoing machine, I never stopped performing live. I prefer to practice continually and strive toward a higher musical goal: the proliferation of my own music. My group goes on the road for a month at a time, affording me the ultimate privilege of being able to challenge myself and reach for it every night. For me, the artistic satisfaction of pulling off a live show is far more rewarding than a day in the studios. So my attitude has become: *There will always be studio work*. I can leave town for six weeks and the Monday I return there will be a session. I don't care about the money I lose or the gigs I have to turn down; I always come back a better player.

I believe this has been the key ingredient to my success. A producer or composer knows if the music is "real" for you. The common misconception of the stereotypical studio musician is that he is a jack of all trades (in this case, styles) but master of none. I prefer to be the master of at least one true thing, to have a personal musical style that is very real to me. Although I enjoy the challenge of various musical styles, I will constantly try to perfect my own, to expand my expertise in a very personal, musical passion, beginning with my tone and progressing all the way through the choice and feel of each note. This commitment is not a job requirement; it's the way I've chosen.

The Evolution of Session Work

In the early years, most studio musicians were jazz guys that looked down on styles like rock, country, and blues. Those styles weren't real to them, and the nickname "hack" or "studio sausage" became commonplace in L.A., especially when describing guitar players. But times began to change for the better. Beginning with Larry Carlton in the mid-'70s, a new wave of players emerged that were very conscious of their tone. New York had a reputation for being a jazz town, and L.A. was the rock town. This was right at the time I entered the scene.

By the mid-'80s, the sounds a guitarist was capable of making rose to a very sophisticated level. We went from pedalboards to racks. Every night I seemed to be reading a manual for a new piece of signal processing gear I had just bought. After a while guitarists unfortunately began to listen to the chorusing and the delay effects more than the actual tone of the guitar. Eventually, I began to rebel against this trend by showing up with a 1961 Strat, a '64 Fender Princeton Reverb, and a few pedals. Today, I have many rigs and combinations of gear that will get the job done. I am a lot less interested in trends and much more interested in the pursuit of my tone.

Changing times have affected the job site as well. Back when I used to do the weekly TV series *Cheers*, there was a contractor, a team of copyists, a music editor, an engineer with his assistants, and a few guys with clipboards running around. We recorded at the cavernous Studio M on the Paramount lot. And this was just for a half-hour sitcom. Now, a similar show is done in somebody's home studio, the composer engineers, a computer prints the music, guitars are overdubbed, and none of those other people are present. These are the economics of the background, or incidental, music you hear on TV and in jingles, but not necessarily records or feature films.

The Studio Scene Today

The advent of inexpensive home recording gear has brought the economics of incidental music way down, and only in very recent years have I seen a trend back toward higher budgets. These days, the big L.A. studios are booked every day. I think we will continue to head in both directions: the big studios will always be there to capture the unique sound of musicians playing together, and home recording will thrive as new technology makes sessions done there even more accepted. Through it all, there will always be music and a need for the artists who create it.

On Gear

The guitars and the gear in the photos throughout this book represent where I am today, at the time of printing, but realize that this is constantly changing and being upgraded. I rarely sell anything, but if there is a better way to make a sound, I want it. You don't need all of this stuff to make a living, but if you do it long enough you'll probably acquire a substantial collection. The main rule is: Don't sell something because it's no longer trendy; if it's good, keep it. I am constantly hearing this sorry phrase: "Damn, I used to have one of those." Well, so did I, and I still do!

Start with your guitar. If it sounds good and you can get around on it, take it to the music store and hear all the amps you can until you find the perfect match. Listen for clarity and a tight (not mushy) low end, both with and without distortion. Your ear will tell you when it's time to move on to different gear, but that doesn't necessarily mean your old stuff is no longer useful. I believe the more amps and guitars you have, the broader your sonic palette will be. And the more sounds you'll have to inspire your music.

I am grateful for the opportunity to share some of these events with you, and I hope you will gain some knowledge from my experience. Realize that this book captures events in a particular time period in my life, with a guitar in my hands eight hours a day. During this time I played on hundreds of sessions, toured six times with my own group and even did six months on the road with Supertramp, a band I joined in 1985.

I hope you enjoy playing through some of the examples and reading the stories that follow. But most of all, I hope it helps you find your way on the guitar.

All the best,
Carl Verheyen
January 2000

From Dusk Till Dawn

Guitar Playing for the Undead

To launch this new column, let me first explain some things about being a studio guitarist. In just the last few years, much of the way we record has changed. More and more, various skills are required that can't really be practiced. Certainly you can practice sight-reading or your rhythm chops, but you can't practice coming up—quickly—with five different parts for a Bm7/E–Em–Fmaj7b5–D+/F♯ progression until you have an impatient producer standing over your shoulder. You also can tweak all of your different sounds at home, but you won't really know how they work with other instruments, or how a studio microphone hears them, until you've listened to dozens of playbacks of yourself. You get this knowledge from working a lot of gigs, going into a lot of different studios, and being prepared for anything.

I did an unusual session a few weeks ago that involved utilizing one of the more elusive guitar skills one needs in the studio: reproducing a specific guitar sound. I was working on the new Quentin Tarantino vampire movie, *From Dusk Till Dawn*, playing surf-guitar overdubs. At one point in the session, the film's music composer, Graeme Revell, asked me if I was familiar with the version of "The Star-Spangled Banner" that Jimi Hendrix played at Woodstock. I replied that yes, I'd been familiar with the piece for the last 26 years, and that like most of Jimi's music, it had a major impact on me as a kid learning to play the guitar. Well, Graeme wanted to use that track in a section of the movie (in the bar scene where the Vietnam veteran reminisces about his tenure there), but it turned out that licensing it for use in the film would be prohibitively expensive. In cases like this, it's cheaper to re-record a famous musical piece and pay a mechanical license on that rather than to license the original. Thus, Graeme wanted me to redo the song and make it sound as close to Hendrix's version as possible.

Besides the sheer fun of attempting such a cool thing, there was an economic bonus to this request. When I did sessions for Steve Martin's *L.A. Story* a few years back, the composer on that movie needed some Django Reinhardt and Stephan Grappelli music re-recorded. My name went down on the union contracts for two sessions (recording and mixdown) as transcriber, copyist, orchestrator/arranger, musician, contractor, guitar player, and leader. I didn't expect all of those credits, but when I got the payment for that movie, my eyes spun like Las Vegas slot machines.

This time, the composer on *From Dusk Till Dawn* offered me free reign as producer. I booked Sunset Sound Recorders, which is where Van Halen's first album was recorded, and where I did some of my newest album, so I knew that the room could get a serious guitar sound.

Now, I'm not a Hendrix historian, but I do have all his records and I've seen *Woodstock* about 20 times, so I had a pretty good idea about the gear that I would need to pull this off. A Univibe, an Octavia, a Fuzz Face, and a wah-wah were all part of Jimi's rig in 1969. I have three Marshall heads (a 1966 JTM-45, a 1968 50-watt, and a 1969 100-watt), so I had them all sent over to Sunset Sound with two late-'60s Marshall 4x12 cabinets outfitted with old Celestion 25-watt greenback speakers. I had my five Fender Strats delivered (which range from 1961 to 1993) because I didn't know exactly which one would give me the most accurate tone.

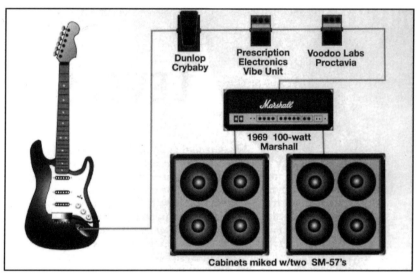

My signal chain for emulating Hendrix's immortal Woodstock performance of "The Star-Spangled Banner."

For pedals, I took a Dunlop Rotovibe and a Vibe Unit by Prescription Electronics. After a few minutes of experimenting with my sound, the Vibe Unit won out. I also had a Proctavia, which is Voodoo Labs' answer to Roger Mayer's old Octavia, and it too sounded just like the record, so I used the distortion in that instead of the Fuzz Face. But I had an old Tube Screamer and a Rat pedal lurking, just in case.

As you might have guessed, the 1969 100-watt Marshall through both bottoms was the perfect amp for the situation, though the '68 50-watt got pretty close. I then tried all my Strats. A maple neck 1987 American Standard worked best for two reasons: The wang bar was adjusted for maximum travel, and I could abuse this guitar rather than mangle one of the vintage axes. I also tuned down a $^{1}/_{2}$ step. Now, even though this session didn't necessarily involve reading, the night before I made myself a free-form chart with no bar lines. I just had eighth notes, quarter notes and half notes interrupted by long arching lines and squiggles that represented the contour of Jimi's divebombs and feedback. In a lot of cases, I also wrote a starting tone to suggest the note from which I should take off. This way, each take would be fairly consistent in case we needed to edit.

The next day, my simple pre-production paid off. I arrived at the studio at 9 a.m., and began choosing amps, pedals, and guitars as my engineer, Bernie Matthews, miked the cabs with close and ambiance microphones. We referenced the *Woodstock* CD a few times, and by 9:30 we were up and ready to record. Since the sound we had was so completely inspiring, we got it in one take (it must have been embedded in my subconscious). We were having so much fun that we decided to go for take 2, but the first one ended up having the real raw energy. By 10:15, we had it mixed and I was on my way to the next session of the day. The guys there couldn't believe we'd just done a Hendrix tune for a major motion picture in less than an hour.

A lot of studio work is "Give me that Mark Knopfler sound" or "It needs that Nirvana feel," but rarely is it fine-tuned or specified to the degree that this session was. On dates like this, it definitely helps to be a fan, because when you're really into it you go the extra mile.

After the gig, I gained a new respect for Jimi's Woodstock performance. Imagine making such a powerful protest statement about the Vietnam War without ever singing a note or speaking a word. Just a guitar. See you next month.

June 1996

Playing Right with the Orchestra

Like most guitar players, I come from a rock and roll background. That's why any chance I get to play with a big orchestra is something I look forward to. A new movie scored by my old friend Craig Safan afforded me such an opportunity.

If you check out the *Cheers* reruns on TV, you'll see in the credits that Craig composed all the music. I played guitar for the last eight years of the show's 12-year run, so my musical relationship with Craig is very trusting. During the course of that show (and on his feature films), he wrote for the guitar in all styles, from jazz to country to hard rock. His imagination knows no bounds, and he's a fearless composer.

For this film I played electric guitar, electric slide, steel-string acoustic, and nylon-string acoustic. To top it off, I played each of them with an 88-piece orchestra. On one particular cue, however, the first 16 bars were an up-front, featured duet between nylon-string guitar and Paraguayan harp, a small ethnic harp with no pedals.

In some ways duets are harder than solos, because you must agree with your partner on feel, time, and pitch. Classical guitars are notoriously "pitchy" (their intonation is suspect) as you get up the neck, and because of the tempo of this piece (around MM=116), I had to play it in the 9th position.

Fortunately, my strings were pretty fresh, so the guitar tuned up nicely with harpist Gayle Levant. Although we were the featured soloists on this cue, we had no extra time to work out our parts. Our first run-through was with all 88 musicians.

On the second half of beat 1 in bar 4, I dropped down to the 7th fret, but jumped back up to the 9th for the rest of the bar. In bar 5, I played beat 1 in 7th position and beat 2 in 5th. After establishing this pattern, I was able to make it work for the rest of the duet section, although bar 13 got pretty high on the neck for a non-cut-away guitar. A seasoned professional, Gayle was able to match my phrasing in terms of staccato and legato notes. She knew the guitar's quirky limitations and adapted accordingly.

In sessions like this, it's a scary moment when you realize that you have the composer, the orchestrator, the conductor, the engineering staff, the studio people, and 88 other musicians listening to your 16 bars, with every one of those musicians poised to come in on the downbeat of bar 17. You're on the edge of your seat anyway, trying to get it right, but it takes serious concentration not to blow bar 15 when you see all those violin bows rise.

The rest of the cue was easy. There was some mariachi-style strumming at bar 47 and after the *grand pause* (everyone rests) at 52, then a lot of counting until bar 68. From there until bar 72 was a four-bar statement of the main title theme, a figure I had already played on electric slide guitar. From bar 74 to the end, we were back to the strumming—however, I was told to play high inversions, and the rhythms had to be dead-on to complement a trumpet part.

There's a Mexican flavor to this movie, so the guitar was featured quite a bit. I really prefer this kind of setup to other orchestral dates I've done with a lot of *tacet* (the guitar lays out) sheets. Sometimes you're the featured soloist, soaring above 75 strings with a Strat and two Marshall cabs (like I was on last year's *Mad Love*) and other times you're just one tiny thread in a huge musical fabric. In all, I'd rather be on the edge of my seat being challenged than sitting around all day. Regardless of the situation, though, the main thing is to keep up your reading chops.

Doubling from a Position of Strength

For some reason that is unknown to me, guitar players are expected to play any musical instrument with strings on it. Besides electric and acoustic six-string guitars, 12-string guitars, slide guitars, nylon-string, dobro, and baritone guitars, we are often asked to play some pretty exotic stringed instruments as well. On various records, movies, and TV dates, I've played electric sitar, four- and five-string banjos, ukulele, tenor guitar (four-string), mandolin, oud, riquinta, and churango. In most of these situations, I was dragged kicking and screaming into it, because normally I just wanna *rock*.

Some of the best studio guys in town have trunks of these instruments, all in guitar tuning (in the tradition of Tommy Tedesco), ready to pounce on these ethnic-sounding tracks with the correct instrument. Although I greatly admire their discipline, at some point along the way, I made the decision to be the best electric and acoustic guitar player I could, and leave the doubling to others. Like I said, I just wanna *rock*.

I did take a few steps over the edge when I bought my first dobro, then a mandolin, and then a couple of banjos. I have all the guitars: 12-strings, classicals, and even a few baritones, but these are instruments that I really want to play. I'm not interested in doing a lot of my own music with balalaikas, ouds, and tiples.

Although television dates can be very "doubling intensive," nobody had ever posed the question, "Carl, how are your bouzouki chops?" That is, not until I was asked recently by composer Jonathan Wolff, an extremely talented and efficient musician who writes much of the quality music you hear on TV. I currently work with him on *Married ... with Children, Boston Common, Unhappily Ever After, Can't Hurry Love, Caroline in the City, Hudson Street,* and *Seinfeld*.

After he asked me the question, I asked him one: "What's a bouzouki?" He said it was "a stringed instrument usually heard in Greek restaurants." I researched it a little further and found that bouzoukis are stringed instruments that have four double courses (sets of strings), like a mandolin, but they are tuned in octaves like a 12-string. Had it been critical, I would have tried to rent or borrow a bouzouki, but this particular Greek-sounding passage was just going to be used as source music.

In TV, "source" is the term that describes music coming from a particular place on the set, like a car radio, a live band, or a home stereo. It's often the best part of the recording session because we generally get to play entire songs instead of four- or five-second cues, which is good if you—have I mentioned this yet?—just wanna *rock*.

The session primarily involved the show's usual country-rock cues, so we decided to "fake" the bouzouki parts with a mandolin and an acoustic 12-string. First, I played a nylon-string guitar rhythm track with the bass and drums, because it seemed like a good "bed."

Next, I went to work overdubbing the melody. This was challenging for two reasons. First reason: tempo. It started at ♩=140 and accelerated to 158 by the end of the third repeat. That's pretty quick for all those 16th notes, especially when you're sight-reading. Second reason: instruments. The mandolin has such tiny frets, accuracy was difficult. And the 12-string was, well, a 12-string. Cumbersome at best.

One of the best tips any teacher ever gave me was about sight-reading, and it came from the late Tony Rizzi. He said, "Always read in a position where the scale pattern lies comfortably under your fingers and requires no stretches or position changes." For example, don't read the key of G in the 5th position; instead, use the 2nd or 7th. It's much easier.

In the music shown here, however, we're dealing with harmonic minor for most of the first half, and I just looked for positions where I could pull it off fast. Bars 1 through 5 were easy enough in the 2nd position, and in bars 6 and 7 I slid up to the 7th position. But in bars 8 and 9, I dropped down to play the E major stuff in the 4th position, where everything lies under your hands. The next four bars (10–13) were split, with the first few notes in 6th position, and the rest of the bar in the 7th. Some of you guys (and gals) with huge hands may play it all in the 5th with stretches, but I find when sight-reading that I can keep it together better when I follow pre-determined position changes (I usually write them on my chart).

From bar 14 to the end, the Tony Rizzi position method made the rest easy. I could have played the lines in 14, 16, 18, 20, and 21 in the 7th position, but 2nd position was better, both for its proximity to the chords and the brightness of the sound.

By the third time through, the accelerando was kicking in, and this baby was flying by! I was happy to find the *fine* at bar 13. At that moment, I realized that there actually was a reason to have your harmonic minor scales together, even if—at the end of the day—you just wanna rock.

Thanks to Jonathan Wolff for writing this chops-munching piece and for hiring me to play it. I probably still won't buy a bouzouki with the drachmas I made on this piece, although some baklava sounds good. See you next month.

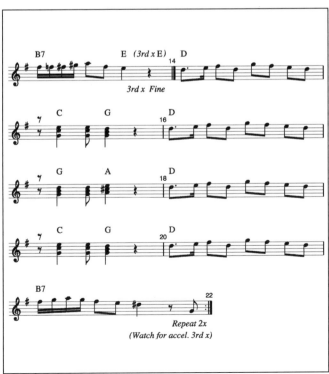

Accidents Will Happen

Golden Moments from Unexpected Events

Sometimes the most magical sounds and tones have come to me purely by accident. All the preparation and pre-production hours you spend tweaking your sound cannot completely prepare you for what happens when you get to the studio. Environmental dynamics in the room probably shape your sound as much as one third, with the other two thirds being your gear and your hands. And time has an influence too.

Why? Because every recording session has a time consideration. It takes a lot of experience to fully grasp this concept. On a TV date or with most jingles, you're expected to be in your chair, in tune, and ready for the downbeat at the session call time. In such a case, the time consideration is *get it done fast*, and they'll more than likely want to be finished in one to three hours. If you're slowing them down, you won't get called back. On the other hand, a record project or movie date can be a lot more relaxed, and if you appear impatient to roll tape, the same thing can happen. Sometimes on an overdub session they'll want to take five hours just to set up the sound.

It is on these occasions that some of the most experimental and interesting tones are produced. A recent experience with this occurred while making my own record.

Unlike my first two records, I wanted this one to be almost completely live. This also suited the music, since it was a very bluesy project. After basic tracking, I gave myself just six days to overdub guitars and vocals, and to mix. (The budget played a major part in this decision.)

By the end of the week, I had about 26 guitars out and around the studio, on stands, on road cases, on the console, on everything. It had been an exciting week of experimenting, and I had one more solo to "carve."

The sound I heard in my head was the most pristine, crystal-clear Strat sound I could find without going direct. I definitely wanted to move some air and get that sweetness on tape, like those early Dire Straits records.

The first thing I went for was my 1965 Fender Stratocaster, because it sounds cleaner than any of the other Strats in my collection. I set my 1964 blackface Fender Princeton Reverb amp up on a stool in the hallway between the live room and the control room and went out to tweak the knobs. We slapped a Neumann U47 tube mic in front of the old Jensen 10-inch speaker, and I headed back into the booth with a long cable, so I could play in front of the monitors.

But on the way to the control room, something amazing happened: I stopped playing as I walked past my Dobro, and I heard the metal cone resonating. It was sitting on a stand 10 feet away, but the sound waves were really bouncing around in there.

I moved the Dobro closer, to a distance of three feet from the Princeton, with every intention of miking it. Then something I had long forgotten came to me: It had a piezo pickup under the bridge! I had purchased the guitar from Jim Messina a few years back, but I had never played it live, so I almost forgot that it could be plugged in.

After getting the best possible guitar sound out of the Princeton, we ran a cable from the Dobro to a direct box, then straight into its own channel on the board (see Figure 1). The sound was completely unique, but I knew it could be even more special after one final adjustment.

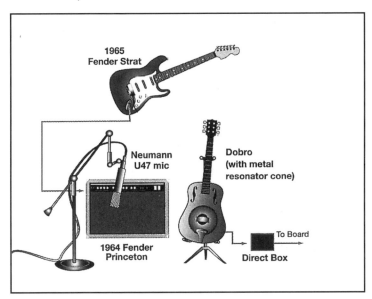

The song I was working on was all diatonic to B♭ major. I used the IV chord, the V chord, and the VIm7 chord, as well as the I chord. For this reason I tuned the Dobro to an open B♭6/9 chord for maximum resonance throughout the entire progression. I think I ended up with F, B♭, D, G, C, F—low to high.

That final tweak made a world of difference, and as I started to play I felt completely inspired. Five minutes later we had a two-and-a-half-minute solo on tape.

The sound was indescribable—like a halo that followed every note. The Dobro reacted differently as I went up or down the guitar neck, sort of like a natural reverb that could be note-specific tuned! Being that the Dobro was on its own channel, we could mix in just the right amount of "angels" to retain the clarity and integrity of the original Strat.

I'm a firm believer in the axiom "If the sound is right, the solo will play itself." Oftentimes we'll spend hours setting up a sound and 15 minutes playing music. But once again, that all-important time-consideration concept comes into play. If you have the time in the studio, experiment.

P.S. The track is called "Silence Is Golden (Part 2)" on my CD *Slang Justice*. Check it out.

The Time Consideration
Sensing the Pace of a Session

A few years ago, I participated in a magazine roundtable discussion with five or six guitar players on the subject of recording work. As we got deeper into the fine points of our profession, Dean Parks said something that I try to remember every time I put on a set of headphones. The interviewer asked what the hardest part of the studio musician's gig is, and Dean said "time consideration." When asked whether that meant having a good time or arriving on time, he replied, "Neither. It means sensing the pace of the session, knowing how much time they want to spend."

I didn't think too much about it then, but as I worked for more producers, contractors, and composers, it began to sink in. Upon your arrival at the studio, you need to make a judgment about the overall speed of the gig. Sometimes they want to burn, like on a TV overdub date where you have half an hour to record all the guitars before the sax player's booking. You check the stack of music on the stand, and make the mental adjustment: These guys want to carve! In that case, you won't be spending time fine-tuning the sound; you need to pave these guitar parts as fast as possible. Poking around with your pedals or spending too much time with a part will ensure that you won't get the call next time.

On the other hand, there are sessions where going too fast can get you fired. Record dates are rarely done in a hurry. If you show up overly anxious to burn, you might rub the producer the wrong way. He and the engineer may have a specific sound in mind, with a budget that allows them to spend all day looking for it. More than likely, however, they won't have anything in mind and they'll want to spend all day hearing everything. If you've never worked for this producer or engineer, you'll find it a bit like walking on eggshells as you try to size up the time consideration.

Record overdubs are always the most tweaky. You might do take after take just trying to dial in the tremolo speed. I've seen them spend hours on mics and mic placement, something that gets pretty tedious when you're good and ready to play. Yet, on some occasions I've recorded entire ten-song albums in a day! Jingles (commercials) are generally quick and dirty. The session is based on a one-hour call, and the length of the music is usually 30 or 60 seconds, so they generally get sounds up pretty quickly. But last month we took three eight-hour days to record the new Taco Bell campaign, so you're never too sure about time until you get there.

As I mentioned, TV music can often be recorded at breakneck speed. Those little sitcoms can take as little as 15 minutes, and an entire Movie of the Week can be done in three to six hours. In these cases, it depends almost entirely on your sight-reading skills; the player dictates the pace. When dealing with television's often-ridiculous deadlines, the faster you can deal with music on the written page, the more valuable you become. Then again, you never know. Recently, I was called to play on the new theme music for *Good Morning America*. Bill Conti, the composer (best known for writing the *Rocky* theme), was very concerned about getting an authentic sound for each of the five musical styles representing the theme. We spent seven hours total recording it—once I sized up the time consideration.

Movie sessions are more like records. Often the music you make becomes a soundtrack album, too. I've often seen the composer and/or conductor spend three hours on the main title, only to re-record it a few days later. On large orchestra dates, the time consideration is usually out of your hands, but it's important to feel the pace of the session.

In every kind of recording work, time consideration is most important when you're overdubbing. If it's a record date, even with just a single song at stake, guitar overdubs can take a while. Oftentimes I'll spend a few moments mapping out the architecture of the song with the artist or producer, as I recently did when working on an album for recording artist Heather Nova (on Sony/Work Records).

The song had a moody intro, almost like a small chamber orchestra tuning up. From there it went verse–chorus–verse–chorus–interlude–verse–chorus–chorus–out. The first thing we agreed on was the chorus. They needed huge power chords sustaining over the bar lines, but definitely not playing eighth notes—too '80s. To achieve a sound, I used my 1970 Les Paul Deluxe (routed for PAFs) through my '68 Plexi Marshall 50-watt, mono through a 4x12 cab. I laid down tracks with that setup, and then doubled them on all four choruses. The sound was big but not quite dense enough, until I added a hot-rod Strat (custom made in 1983 by Renson Guitars), with a Lindy Fralin humbucker through a Rat pedal. I used the same Marshall with this guitar.

Now it was time to concentrate on the verses. For contrast, we decided a "small" sound was appropriate, so I played my Chandler Strat-style guitar with lipstick-tube pickups through an old blackface Fender Tremolux head. The tremolo on the amp wasn't deep enough for the quirky part, so I used the Voodoo Labs tremolo pedal, dialing the speed to the song's tempo. We then printed this part on all three verse sections.

For the instrumental interlude, the producer wanted something different than a solo, so I ended the three-hour session playing a non-pitched, percussive wah-wah part for eight bars. A few days later, I got another call from Heather's producer saying the song really needed a bluesy solo, more stuff in the choruses, and something in the intro. Over my wah-wah guitar, I played some jagged little blues lines with my '54 Les Paul gold-top (with P-90s) through an Electroplex Rocket 90 head and an old Fender Bandmaster bottom. We took a long time to arrive at this combination of gear, but the solo sound was worth it.

With my Ramirez nylon string, I played a weird tremolo figure in the intro and then doubled it (in the chamber orchestra section). Using a '60 Telecaster, I played a clean melodic hook over all that grunge in the choruses, which helped elevate it beyond the overused Nirvana formula. Finally, I added screaming feedback to the last chorus (with my '61 Strat through a '69 100-watt Marshall) to give it a little lift.

It ended up being ten tracks of guitars in seven hours, but it just as easily could have been one track in one hour. The joy of creativity makes this job one of the best in the world. All it takes is a little patience, concentration, and time consideration.

P.S. I found out later that the Heather Nova song I've described will be heard instrumentally in the new *Crow* movie sequel, *City of Angels*. It will be released with the vocal on the European soundtrack CD, and domestically on the Hollywood Records movie soundtrack. Sometimes you never know where your studio work will end up.

Acoustic Tricks

The Importance of the Capo

In the last two weeks, I've worked on three different projects using nothing but acoustic instruments. Two of them were record projects and one was a jingle, but the universal lesson to be learned here applies to all three sessions.

Recently I changed my cartage trunks so that one case holds only acoustics and a few related stringed instruments. This is handy when a producer or composer wants options. If you were to show up for a record date with only one six-string acoustic, it might not be the sound they're looking for. Some acoustics are sweet sounding, like a Martin D-28. Others are better for strumming big open chords, like a Guild F-50. And others rock, like Gibsons—they seem to self-compress as if Keith Richards was flogging away.

What's important to recognize here are the properties of the acoustic guitar, and that you should approach it differently than the electric. (This may sound very basic, but I'm always amazed at how many players don't know how to deal with acoustic guitars.) Consider this progression (Example 1) in the key of B♭ major. The first thing I notice is that the key is very acoustic-unfriendly, especially if we want to showcase what I consider to be the instrument's most important quality: open strings. This is where the capo, an important tool, comes in handy. (I even have the appropriate capo for each acoustic guitar.) Placing the capo on the third fret puts the entire progression in the key of G major, giving you many more open strings and acoustic licks, but

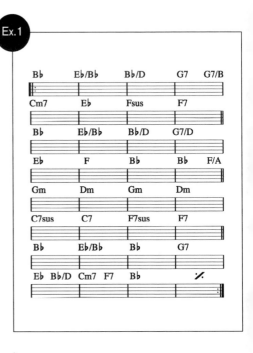

Ex.1

B♭	E♭/B♭	B♭/D	G7	G7/B
Cm7	E♭	Fsus	F7	
B♭	E♭/B♭	B♭/D	G7/D	
E♭	F	B♭	B♭	F/A
Gm	Dm	Gm	Dm	
C7sus	C7	F7sus	F7	
B♭	E♭/B♭	B♭	G7	
E♭ B♭/D Cm7 F7	B♭		%.	

how quickly can you transpose? Will you hold up the entire rhythm section while you write down all the changes in the new key? And what if they change keys?

Early on I had a teacher who made me harmonize the major scale. I wrote out the C scale, then built a chord on each degree using thirds. The stack of notes over each scale tone is the harmonized major scale, with all the chords being diatonic to that key (Example 2). That little bit of music theory has been one of the most useful things I ever learned, because I apply it every day in one form or another.

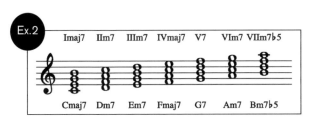

The next thing this teacher had me do was harmonize the major scale in all 12 keys. When I questioned the redundancy of such a time-consuming exercise, he shot back with the question, "Okay, what's the vim7 chord in D♭?" When I hesitated for a few moments, picturing a guitar neck and counting frets, he said, "That's why. This information should be second nature to all musicians."

The next step is to assign a number system to each chord. You've heard of the I–IV–V progression; that sort of notation is an example of the number system concept. In some sessions I've done, chord symbols were abolished in favor of numbers so that the band could move easily from one key to another to accommodate a singer. This is most common in Nashville studios. The faster you are able to deal with the number system, the better you will be at transposition.

Next month, I'll show you how this works when you're on the clock and under the gun during a session.

Acoustic Tricks, Part 2

Playing by the Numbers

Last month I talked about working with acoustic guitars during a session, and the need to be able to deal with the idiosyncrasies of the instrument, especially open strings and transposing using a number system. Let's revisit the progression I was playing. See Example 1.

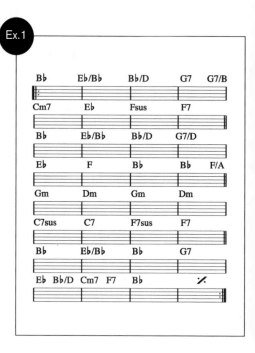

Ex. 1

We start with the I chord to the IV chord with the I chord's root in the bass. Back to the I chord with the 3rd in the bass to the VI dominant chord. The second half of the bar has the 3rd in the bass, which resolves to the IIm7 chord. This is followed by the IV chord and the Vsus to the V dominant. Looking at this in the key of G major it becomes:

| G | C/G | G/B | E7 E7/G♯ | Am7 | C | Dsus | D7 ‖

The second eight-bar section is very similar but with a slightly different turnaround. This leads to an eight-bar bridge. Using the number system, the bridge looks like this:

| vi | iii | vi | iii | II7sus | II7 | V7sus | V7 ‖

In the key of G, those numbers translate into simple open chords, which allow the ringing strings to sparkle in the track.

In this particular song, I was asked to do a fingerpicking part in the James Taylor tradition. For this I used an acoustic guitar handmade by luthier Mark Angus of

Long Beach, California, because intricate parts always sound great on this instrument. I've always been a fan of the first Joni Mitchell album, which was produced by David Crosby. On most of the tracks, they doubled the guitar.

After doubling it from top to bottom with a 1957 Gibson J-50, I was given a new challenge: Make it build. I suggested the acoustic 12-string, capoed at the 8th fret, strumming the downbeats of each bar from the second verse on. For this part we needed to transpose to the key of D, and play it on the 10th fret. My Taylor acoustic 12-string sounded great up there—almost like a harpsichord if miked correctly. Once again, we got some great open chords: The E♭ became a G chord, the G7 became a B7, the Cm7 became an Em7, and the F7 became an A7.

Using the number system to transpose, I came up with this part instantly, and "paved" it on the first run through. The producer could now choose where and when to bring it in at the mix.

Now the track was beginning to take on a more orchestrated sound. I suggested some slide guitar, and we decided to use a dobro. Since I keep mine set up with pretty high action for playing slide, a capo was out of the question. So I tuned the instrument to an open E♭ chord, giving me the I chord at the 7th fret. This can get pretty complicated unless you use the number system, because B♭ is on the B♮ fret! I kept the part fairly simple, and stayed out of the bridge entirely (minor chords are tough in a major chord–based tuning). At one point I tried a G tuning on an acoustic guitar, capoed at the 3rd fret, but we got too much fret noise with the slide, and the dobro offered a completely different sound.

There were still many more possibilities that we didn't try because—except for the solo—this track sounded done. I regret not having a low E♭ bass note anywhere except in the dobro part. I could have devised a tuning to accommodate that like Richard Thompson does, or maybe strung up a baritone acoustic with my low E voicing sounding B♭ major. (I have an electric bari tuned to B, so this is not too much of a stretch.) But at some point the producer always says, "That's enough, Carl—down boy."

For the solo, which was just the eight bars of bridge changes, I used a 1938 Gibson L-00. It's one of those small-body guitars with a character all its own. Because of its small size, it is voiced differently than my other instruments, so it really cuts through the track and sounds like a solo.

We ended up with five tracks: two unison fingerpicking guitars for a left and right stereo bed, the 12-string strumming downbeats real high up the neck, the dobro for color, and the solo. The only reason I don't mention who the artist was on this session is because I know they are trying a few other versions, and I don't know if mine will end up on the CD. The last I heard, there was a string quartet version, a band version, and a synth-keyboard version! But we all know the guitar version is going to sound best.

It's All Relative

Pitch Peril

Because I wasn't born with perfect pitch, I've always worked hard on my relative pitch. This is something you can practice away from the guitar, and it's one of the most important studies for getting in tune with your instrument. I've had a number of experiences—some good, some bad—that have made it obvious just how important good ear-training skills are.

I ran myself through an ear-training practice regimen for 12 years. Whenever driving in my car, alone or with friends, I would attempt to name the key of the song on the radio, and then I'd check it using a pitch pipe. After a while it became easy, especially if I had already played guitar that day. Soon I was hearing all the chord changes going by and imagining what the melody would look like on paper. My relative pitch became much more developed the more I worked at it, and my overall playing became stronger because I could hear lines and chords in my head before I played them.

Once you get into the pitch-pipe-in-the-car groove, you can work on intervals while driving. Play an A natural, and attempt to sing the 6th above it or the ♭5 below. Soon you'll be able to do takedowns in real time and hear all the intervals in your head. I once asked a brilliant big-band composer, "Did you write this composition on the guitar or the piano?" He replied, "On the couch." It occurred to me that he had a highly trained ear and sense of pitch, so he didn't need an instrument to know what his music would sound like. I have always aspired to that goal.

However, recently I was called to play on a few rock and roll tracks for an upcoming Warner Bros. movie entitled *Carpool*. For two days I had been very sick with a fever and a sore throat, but I accepted the date thinking that by Wednesday, I'd be over this nasty flu. But on the morning of the session I woke up with a 101-degree fever and still had to go to work.

The session was fairly easy—guitar, bass, and drums. Phil Marshall, the composer, provided us with chord charts and a few lines to play, and we breezed through the first song in two takes. By this time, however, I was feeling really bad, and started to get dizzy.

I pulled out a '60 Telecaster Custom for the next piece, and the only thing strange that I remember was the bass player saying, "Wow, let me tune to you." The verse changes were something like D to B for eight bars and the chorus went to G major. We slammed it out and I doubled the rhythm guitar before moving on to the third and final track. I was so sick. I remember thinking, "I just have to get through this one last overdub and then I'm done." I actually started to feel better with all the vitamin C, Sudafed, liquids, etc., that I was pounding, but when I got home and took my temperature, it was 104 degrees! I went straight to bed.

Around 4:00 that afternoon, in my delirious stupor I got a call from Phil, the composer. He said, "You won't believe it, but your Tele was tuned a half step down and you played the second song in D♭ instead of D. When we put up the pre-recorded vocals, they were a half-step off!" I guess I was so sick that 32 years of ear training went right out the window, and I must have misread the lights on my tuner.

So I was lying in bed with a 104-degree fever and he asked me to come back to the studio and re-do those tracks. There was no way—I was totally out of it. I told them to take the Eventide H-3000 out of my rig (which was still at the studio) and harmonize the track up a half step. Meanwhile, I called around looking for a guitar player who could blaze down to Hollywood, plug into my gear, and carve.

When the dust finally settled, it appeared that the deadline was a bit looser, so I ended up going back two days later and replacing those tracks. I also re-cut a solo on another song. It's amazing how much better you play when you feel good. Of course, I didn't charge Warner Bros. for the extra session—all work guaranteed! And I still can't believe I didn't hear the difference between D and D♭. I was useless and weak. Totally wiped out!

My reason for relating this sad tale to you: You can never be too prepared. Also, I realized that for the last six months I've been telling you how great I played on this record or that soundtrack, or whatever. So this month is about how lame I played on something. Time to put the pitch pipe back in the car.

Suddenly Soundtracked

Beethoven on a Sitcom

Summertime is usually the time when all the new TV shows are frantically trying to finalize the music for their main titles. The composer's life gets crazy as he makes yet another demo of the many changes the network puts the music through. The guitar player, on the other hand, plugs in, reads it down, and goes on to his 11 a.m. session stress free!

This particular show was interesting because the main title was Beethoven's "Ode to Joy" done in 4/4 rock and roll style. The tracking date used two guitar players (Dean Parks and myself). Bernie Dresell played drums, with Dave Marotta on bass. There was also a percussionist, Brian Kilgore. Our fearless composer, Ed Alton, besides scoring all the cues, had the task of arranging this well-known classical piece for loud rock guys.

Therefore, he purposely did what any Beethoven lover would do: he wrote six guitar parts. Without worrying about who plays guitar one or two, we divided up the parts. Dean played the very top line, which was the main theme. The melody in bars 8–10 was interesting because it was a lick I did in one of the original demos that got transcribed to the final version, and he read it down as if it were his own. We dialed in complementary sounds—I think I used a 1970 Les Paul Deluxe (with a pair of Gibson PAFs added later) through a 1968 Plexi 50-watt Marshall. I used this sound for the harmony line (line #2).

Then we divided up line #3. The first two bars are electric 12-string, and from bar 5 on it's a screaming high lead guitar answering the main theme. Dean played the 12-string part (the trick was getting those high voicings in tune) and I did the answers. For a contrasting tone, I changed to a '61 Fender Strat and a THD amp head. I went for the back pickup and fired up my RAT pedal.

This finished up the electrics, and then it was time to "pave" some acoustics. By this time the rhythm section was gone, so we set up for a real nice acoustic sound. Normally I use thin picks for my strumming parts, but on this track, since there were bass lines to double, I used a heavy.

When all of this was completed, we did a 20-second version of the same piece (I think we switched parts to keep it interesting!). Like most TV and motion picture work, you're under a serious time crunch. Therefore, even though the music was extremely easy to read (even at ♩=182), the pace of the session is where the difficulty comes in. If you bend a note sharp or flat, especially in the two-guitar harmony sections, you have to redo it or punch it in. If you just read it down with no personality it sounds lifeless, so the trick is to make it sound like you've been playing this song all your life. Tone, intonation, time, phrasing, and sight-reading are all the subtleties that need to be dealt with before you walk through those doors. When the red light goes on, it's time to carve.

Supervibe

Finding the Hook in Every Part

Because the last two months have been a musical blur, I will try to distill a few guitar playing tips from all the hours I've put in between the headphones.

My main project was a Supertramp record, which has been an enormous under-taking. It involved two weeks of pre-production rehearsal with the band, three weeks of tracking (six days a week, eight hours a day), and two weeks of guitar overdubs. Having toured with the group in the mid-'80s, it was a great reunion of old friends, and a creative camaraderie was enjoyed by everyone involved.

I learned many subtle things aboard this juggernaut. A band that's been around as long as Supertramp, and a producer who's been around as long as Jack Douglas (Aerosmith, Cheap Trick, John Lennon), have by now developed defin-itive ways of doing things. As a player, this meant re-thinking a few concepts.

First, I realized that the most important aspect of playing on the basic tracks was creating a vibe. I would show up at the studio with all my parts for a particular song sorted out into, say, a basic pass plus three or four overdubs. But just play-ing the basic pass didn't convey the vibe. I learned it was more important to track the combination of all the parts, including the guitar solo, so that the bass and drums set up the musical sections (verse, chorus, bridge, etc.) with conviction.

Oftentimes this meant that nothing I played on the basic was a keeper. During the overdubs, we would sort out the various parts and spend all the time need-ed to get the perfect sound for each guitar, but the basic was about the vibe. This was somewhat of a departure from my normal, efficient way of working.

When the tracking was over, it was time to concentrate on detail. The producer and engineer transferred our working masters (culled from 90+ reels of two-inch, 24 track analog tape) to digital tape. We overdubbed guitars, vocals, keyboards, horns etc. to this format and began building the songs and working out the parts.

It's pretty typical to find yourself spending a long time setting up the sound and much less time performing. On one track I played my 1958 Gibson ES-175 jazz guitar through a Leslie, using the warm, fuzzy tube amp in the Hammond organ to drive it. The next section of the same song called for my old '60 Telecaster on the bridge pickup through the normal channel of one of my '63 Vox AC30s. The top boost AC30 sound was about as far away as you could get sonically from the Gibson-Leslie combo, but it worked.

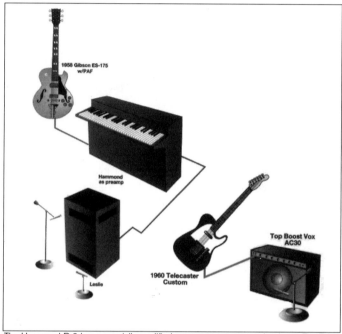

The Hammond B-3 has a specially modified preamp to accept a guitar input. The Tele was put through the Normal Channel of the Top Boost AC30.

In this situation, one must operate under the basic idea that every part is a hook. Even the simplest rhythm guitar part should add a tangible and identifiable cog to the wheel. Oftentimes this involves a lot of thinking and listening away from the guitar. I stress this because our hands are accustomed to a catalog of rhythm guitar licks that we automatically call upon when we see Am7, for example, or any familiar progression.

This concept also applies to solos. Because we all work towards a certain virtuosic ideal in our improvising, it comes as a shock when you're actually in the moment with an amazing sound, ready to carve your lasting statement on this tune, and everyone is telling you to simplify. But in the pop-rock world, where every part is a hook, every guitar solo must be singable. Technique and chops take a back seat to melody and invention. And ego is not in the picture at all. It's far more important in the overall picture to have a huge number of people singing your solos, instead of a small number of guitar players raving about your hammer-ons!

More about sounds and gear next month. . . .

Power Chords Only
No Triads Need Apply

Recently I got a call for a record date that was unusually specific: "We want power chords only. No need for an extensive guitar rack system—just crunch." The group was the Bee Gees, a band that's been producing hits since the '60s. The producer seemed to have a severe case of rack-a-phobia (an aversion to extensive racks, brought about by an overexposure to fake-sounding guitar rigs in the late '80s). I have no problem with that. Although my rack gear has been updated, re-tooled, and fine-tuned for the current trends in music, I'm perfectly happy to leave that stuff at the warehouse and work with amp heads, speaker cabs, and combos. Records are usually done that way: You produce a natural, great-sounding guitar tone and the engineer provides the effects. I always ask for a little reverb, to make it comfortable to play in the room. Remember, no matter how many rack-mounted effects you bring, they can always do it better from the control room when it comes to reverb and even delay.

So I showed up with eight heads and three combos, two trunks of guitars, some pedals, and two 4x12 Marshall cabinets. When the producer said that the studio looked like a mini NAMM show with all my gear in it, I reminded him that we were doing power chords, and there are many different sounds available in that corner of guitar playing.

The first thing that comes to mind, probably the universal standard, has to be the Les Paul through a Marshall. Not only is it the sound, but it's a combination often asked for by name by many producers, songwriters, and even film composers. Most solid-body guitars with a humbucker in the bridge position will get that sound, but there's nothing quite like the real thing.

However, there are many other options. Single-coil pickups on Strats and Teles have a unique power chord sound. And they do the "semi-distorted" tone much better than humbuckers, allowing the sometimes-necessary inclusion of 3rds in the chords. A Telecaster rear pickup can produce a raunchy crunch with a bite. A Strat in the middle position (center pickup) has a certain glassy quality to it. The two back pickups together have a completely different, almost hollow sound when distorted. P-90s are different still—warmer than the Fenders, but without the full steam of a humbucker. Filter 'Trons, the pickups in a Gretsch 6120, offer yet another tone resulting from the combination of a real bright pickup in a hollow-body guitar.

That brings me to amps. Sometimes a unique distortion comes from an amp that wasn't meant to do that, like a Fender Tremolux, Bassman, or Concert, or a Vox AC30 or AC15. I generally stay away from master-volume amps when recording, preferring the sound of the power tubes working overtime. These lower-watt amps can deliver a very natural tone, especially the old tweed and blackface Fender stuff.

Sometimes, producers aren't even thinking about distortion when they ask for power chords. What they want is a strong chord with no 3rd, so that the harmony is not specific to major or minor. The term *power chord* most often translates to a two-note dyad consisting of the root and the 5th. On charts you'll often see it notated as D5 or even "D power" (see Example 1).

As you can see, there are a number of tonal options. I listened to the track for the session, and after trying a few things we settled on a stereo pair: a '69 Thinline Telecaster through a '66 Marshall 50-watt on one side, and, strangely enough, a '65 Rickenbacker 12-string (with a little hair on it) on the other. I think I used a THD head for that. The blend was great; the two guitars complemented the track perfectly and worked well together. Another interesting thing was the voicings. I ended up playing "2 chords" or "sus2" voicings (see Example 2). Though it was an uncommon response to a request for power chords, it worked, partially because these voicings aren't specific to major or minor either.

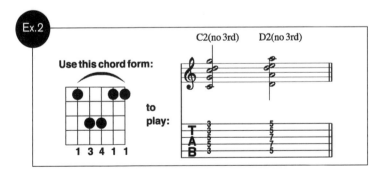

Those voicings wouldn't work with the typical Les Paul/Marshall configuration, so in the end, the producer was very happy with all those options, and I was given another great opportunity to experiment with the tools of tone.

I never got to meet the Bee Gees, but I heard they really liked the track. It sure didn't sound like disco after the power chords went on there!

33

The Big Three

Answers to the Triumvirate of Burning Questions

This month, I thought I would answer the three questions I'm asked more than any others. Every time I do a clinic or a live gig, aspiring musicians ask the same questions I was asking 20 years ago. Although the times have changed, the answers remain pretty much the same.

1 **"How do you break into the studio scene?"**
The answer for each one of us will be different because we're all starting from different places, but the common thread for all musicians is networking. Whether you're playing wedding receptions, parties, clubs, touring, or teaching, it's important to seek out the best players in every situation, exchange numbers, and keep in touch. Players you meet in the lamest situations may turn out to be on their way up and may eventually recommend you to a composer or producer with a real gig. Look for the talented guys who are too hip for the room. I met my good friend Brad Cole (who is now Phil Collins' keyboardist and has played on hundreds of records, including two of mine) on a tennis court in Beverly Hills, playing at someone's backyard party. I've met other players in local clubs, on the road, and, of course, in the studio. Eventually your name gets around, your reputation spreads, and you get associated with quality work. But it does take time.

2 **"How important is reading music in the studios these days?"**
Reading is every bit as important now as it was 20 years ago. Studio time is expensive, projects have deadlines, and budgets are strict. All this points to the fact that in today's competitive music business, no one has the time to wait for the guitar player to learn his or her part. It just takes one session where the bass, drums, keyboards, harmonica, saxophone, and trumpet player are nailing their parts and you're busy counting ledger lines or trying to tap out the *and* of 3 with your foot. (You get it together quickly after that.) And the scary thing is that even the gigs that don't require a serious sight-reader are generally given to readers because they are the ones who can get it together the fastest. It's all about communication.

When we are hired as sidemen, we are expected to fulfill a musical need that is communicated to us by the leader of the date. It may be conveyed to us in the form of treble clef notes, bass clef notes, chord symbols in bar lines, the number system on the back of a napkin, bar lines with no chords or notes and just dynamic markings, or even staff 12 of an entire score. Experience prepares you much better than practice, but you'll need to have a certain amount together before you get in the door. Last year I was doing a session for Stewart Copeland (former drummer for the Police, currently into film composing). I was given a chart in bass clef (not my strongest clef) to play on five-string banjo (not my axe). The banjo tunes to an open G with the bottom string being the highest note, so sight-reading on it was out of the question. The only solution: Transpose, retune, and make it happen. The only thing that got me through that date was experience and confidence, because nothing in my pre-professional practice and training prepared me for that.

One more thing about reading: Although I consider it an asset to any guitar player's hireability, I also consider it a privilege to be able to tap into the mind of another musician and hear what he heard while creating it. Wake up on a Sunday morning and play something from Bach's violin sonatas and partitas. You're in for a very rich experience checking out firsthand the counterpoint, polyphony, and harmony of these little artistic gems exactly as Bach intended them. They'll inspire your writing, elevate your improvising, and urge you to study a different kind of music. Reading helps everything.

 "How much gear do I need to start out?"
You certainly don't need dozens of instruments to get started. In fact, you might already own the basics:
1) A versatile electric guitar, capable of clean tones and distortion
2) An amplifier matched to your main electric guitar
3) Some processing gear for chorus, tremolo, etc.
4) Wah-wah, volume, and distortion pedals
5) A steel-string acoustic
6) A nylon-string acoustic

Eventually you'll be called to play 12-string acoustic and electric, slide electric and acoustic, dobro, baritone guitar, etc. Borrow them at first to make the session, but go out and buy the instrument as soon as you get paid for the gig. My gear-buying philosophy: Always buy the best possible stuff you can afford. That way when you can afford a better one you'll have no problem selling the first one! And don't sell anything that sounds good—you'll always regret it.

They Ride Again

Saddle up Those Acoustic Guitars

The other day while channel surfing, I happened upon a rerun of a western-oriented TV show from the early '90s. I was just about to change channels when this guitar groove caught my ear, and I realized it was me and two other local lads, John Goux and John Wheelock. So I dug around in the closet and came up with a few cues that I had collected from those sessions. This one, "3M6," has a lot going on in 32 bars . . . so let's take it apart.

For starters, this one piece of music is for two players, one on six-string acoustic and the other on dobro switching to nylon string. I played the two-guitar part. At the top of the piece, we get four free clicks in our headphones out in front of bar 1, and then we play nothing! That bar of rest is probably because someone else—the trumpet, violin, or harmonica—had a solo figure there.

In bar 2, the six-string acoustic enters. That little squiggle over the B♭ note means you bend it up to C♮. In bar 3, the short line over the B♭ means that although it's only an eighth note, we play it as long as possible. Likewise, the legato slur over bar 4 indicates the entire phrase is to be played smoothly.

In bar 7, the dobro joins the six-string, sliding into the low C, but not for long. The time signature has changed to 2/4 and it's tied over to a bar of 3/4. Now, here's where it gets interesting. In bar 8, the symbol above the staff is a *fermata*. This instructs us to sustain the note until the conductor cuts us off. In this case, however-er, the click went away, and we waited for two free clicks in a new, much faster tempo before launching into bar 9.

The two-bar figure beginning at 9 is for both six-string acoustic and dobro (with-out the slide). In beats 2 and 3, the copyist has used slash marks as a shortcut to avoid writing out the four 16th notes two more times. But we play the low C 16th notes for three beats, with the accent on the first 16th. This is evident from the accent notation, the sideways "V," and the slur mark over the last two notes in bar 9, which indicates a hammer-on to me. Bar 10 has accent marks and staccato marks (the small dots over the notes). It's especially important to get phrasing indications like these right when two players' parts are in unison.

In the next six bars (11 through 16), we repeat that two-bar figure, and in bar 17 we play it up a 4th. This is evident by *sim.*, an abbreviation for *simile*, which means, "continue in a similar fashion."

When it drops down a whole step in bar 18, we probably played the second half of the phrase for continuity. This entire section was probably played around ♩=126, which is typical chase scene tempo.

When we hit the C (no 3rd) in bar 20, we interpreted the arrow to strum from low to high. I had to set the dobro down silently to my left while reaching for the nylon-string on my right. It's a bit of choreography, but at the end of the 5/4 bar there's another fermata, which bought me a little time. And the two free clicks are into a slower tempo, so it's not that hard to make the change.

Beginning in bar 22, the nylon plays slowly and expressively. The opening triplet is tied into a slash mark, which means to let those three notes ring together as a chord before playing the 3rds on beat 4. In bar 24, I'm instructed to strum the 3rds, which really make the passage sound Spanish. The 16th-note triplet in bar 26 is also ground-zero Spain; it sounds like the *Concierto de Aranjuez* by Rodrigo.

The first time you sight-read bars 29 and 30, you probably won't notice that it's just a Cm barre chord at the 8th fret. My 4th finger reaches up for the E♭ on beat 2 of bar 30, but I don't usually trust the intonation on a nylon-string above the 12th fret. So I played the high G as a harmonic on the 3rd string, 5th fret.

Now it's time to check out a few dynamic markings. The *mp* under bar 2 stands for *mezzo piano*, which means "half-soft" or moderately soft. When the chase scene begins in bar 9 we get much louder, as indicated by *ff*, which means . . . double *forte*. At bar 21, there is a *diminuendo* or gradual decrease in volume to another *mp* dynamic in 22. The word *molto*, written under the diminuendo marking, means "very" . . . so we get quiet very quickly.

The word "solo" over bar 29 doesn't mean I get to blow for two bars. In this case it indicates that I'm playing those last two bars alone. Notice in bar 30 another diminuendo and the Italian *piu meno*, which means "less."

There's nothing difficult about this chart, but there is a lot of information on the page, and I hope I've made it seem a bit clearer to you. Thanks to John Debney for allowing me to use his music. It was a fun show and a good band. We'll ride again!

Time on the Dime
Writing Music to Fit

I write this month's column from 30,000 feet in the air, as I am heading to Europe with my band for a three-week tour. We begin in Copenhagen, Denmark, and will work our way down through Germany, Belgium, and the Netherlands. I feel very fortunate to have the opportunity to play my own music for the next 18 gigs. Besides being the most challenging thing I do, it's also the most therapeutic. That first note onstage in a responsive room washes away all those tedious hours of being a worker-bee sideman. (Like those days when the bass player and drummer are out in the lounge drinking coffee and making phone calls, and the producer says, "Just one or two more guitar overdubs before we move on to the next song.")

But on a few sessions last week, I was not only that worker-bee sideman, but that slave-driving producer as well. I had taken on a writing (and recording) assignment for a music production library. (Library music is that relentless rock and roll you hear under TV sports shows, or shows like *Hard Copy* and *Extra*. It's even used as source music on sitcoms and dramatic shows.) My gig was to write ten two-minute rock pieces in various styles ranging from grunge to surf.

Most of you out there who play in bands will probably never need to know how to write a song that is exactly two minutes long, but you may find the assignment interesting. It's also the same formula they use to make a jingle time out to exactly 60 seconds. It's the same formula film composers use to make the whole orchestra hit a triple *forte* stab when the bad guy jumps out from under the stairs.

It works like this: As you begin formulating the musical idea that will become your main groove or melody, you select a tempo. A metronome will do, but I use an Alesis SR-16 drum machine because the 50 preset patterns are fun to play with. Once you come up with the optimum tempo for your song, you divide 60 by your tempo. This gives you your beat length in seconds—the actual length of each beat.

Let's say my tempo is 106. I divide 60 by 106 and come up with a beat length of .566 seconds, or a little more than half a second. Now, since my assignment was to write a two-minute song, I divide 120 seconds (two minutes) by .566. This figure will be the number of beats in a two-minute song at $\quarternote$=106 tempo. The number is

212, which we then divide by four (since we're in 4/4 time) to find the number of bars in the tune. We get 53 bars—an odd number, but there are many musical solutions: a one-bar drum fill at the top, a five- or seven-bar bridge. In my case, I subtracted a measure from the piano solo.

Knowing that the entire song needs to be 53 bars (including reverb ringout), I simply map it out and work backwards. Since the A section repeats, I've got eight bars at the top. The B section is a five-bar phrase, bringing me to 13 bars. I keep adding up the measures right through the guitar solo at letter E. That brings me to 45 bars so I D.S. (repeat back to the sign) to pick up another five bars before taking the three-bar coda. Exactly 53 bars. I leave a technical note on the track sheet that the reverb is to last three beats and be "off on one" of the next bar.

To get a 30-second version of this song, I would divide 30 by .566 and get 53. This is the number of beats in a 30-second song at our 106 tempo. Divide that by four and I get 13.25, which are 13 bars and one quarter note. Now I work backwards to bring the essential vibe of the song off in 13 1/4 bars. I could start with a bar of drums and play four bars of the A section, then play letter B and take the coda. That gives me 13 bars—but I'll need one extra quarter note, so I'll extend the 'verb out to beat 2 of bar 14 at the end.

It's as simple as that. When a film composer scores a dramatic scene, he uses the formula not only for determining the length of the cue, but also to nail the "hit points" in the scene. And the jingle guys use it to make a 60-, 30-, or 15-second version of their "McDonald's" song. (That's why they always drop a bar out of a song you've heard all your life, like Aretha Franklin's "Respect.")

But the most important thing about composition is the residuals. I get paid a "sync" fee and a BMI residual every time this song is used on TV. I call it "horizontal money"—the bread you make while you're sleeping. Or, in my case, while I'm on the other side of the world saying, "Hello Berlin, it's good to be back."

Creative Phrasing When Sight-reading

Yesterday was a typical day in the studios: two TV dates and a jingle. These kinds of gigs are the meat and potatoes of a recording musician's daily workload. They pay the bills, keep the health insurance hours topped off, and generally keep the chops up—even if they are not as creative as record dates or movie projects.

But the creativity comes in other ways. The music shown here is the opening cue for the new season of a TV show. We do the music in the composer's home studio, and the two guys that write it—Scott Gale and Rich Eames—are good friends of mine, so the last nine years have been pretty fun.

The general vibe of this show has been energetic rock. I usually use one sound the whole time: a Strat through a Mesa/Boogie studio preamp direct into the board, with the gain on about 2 1/2. There isn't the need, budget, or space for my big rig, so direct recording works fine for this gig.

Where the creativity comes in is in the phrasing. Remember that one of the hardest things about sight-reading music is to make it sound like you're not sight-reading. It should sound like you've been playing the part for 20 years.

The first bar is a typical blues-bending lick in 3rd position. The arrows before beats 1, 2 1/2, and 3 1/2 indicate 3rd-string bends, Chuck Berry style. On beat 4 1/2, I slide up to the 5th position for the A and C, dropping down a fret for the B and A. The first two beats of bar 3 are played in 5th position, but I hit the E♮ as an open string to give me the time to switch down to open position for the B through G sequence at the end of the bar. By bending the B slightly flat at beat 3, I get more of a "Honky Tonk Women" vibe out of the line. This is a perfect example of knowing what the composers want to hear and delivering it.

Another rule of thumb is to search out the guitaristic rock licks and play them in the positions and with the phrasing you normally do. Bar 4 has a typical major-pentatonic line that I played in the 5th through 7th positions. I ended it with a bend anticipating the downbeat of bar 5, and I probably bent the A on beat 3, too.

The rest of it is pretty straight-ahead. I overdubbed the rhythm part playing eighth notes with a slightly distorted crunch tone. The last bar is anticipated by a quarter note, so you almost need to treat bar 7 as a bar of 3/4.

This is pretty simple stuff. If you heard it once, you'd be able to nail it. The trick is to nail it the first time, before you've heard it. We burn through about 30 of these cues—rhythm and lead, harmony parts, alternate endings (with rhythm and lead)— and a couple of five-minute source cues in one three-hour session, so there's no time to rehearse your parts. Many times the initial run-through pass becomes the take, because the red light is always on.

The strangest aspect to all of this struck me when I was on the road with my band and I turned on the TV in Denmark. I heard myself soloing madly, and when the tube lit up, it was the TV show and the voices were dubbed in Danish! A week later I heard another one in Germany, and there was the music we recorded in a garage in Santa Monica, California! The world gets smaller every day.

August 1997

Variety
Keeping Things Interesting

Today at 7 a.m. I was awakened by a phone call from an interviewer at a French magazine called *Guitar and Bass*. After a lengthy discussion about my latest record, *Slang Justice*, he asked me, "What is the best thing about your day gig as a freelance studio guitar player?"

The answer to that question can be summed up in just one word: variety. Imagine a job where each day you work in a different environment with different people. I do see a lot of the same faces month to month, but not enough to get tired of them. And although I look forward to some studios more than others, the level here in L.A. has to be one of the highest in the world, and the sessions never last too long before I'm on my way to the next one.

In this business, every project is its own animal. You can work on a hard rock record one day and a children's record the next. You can spend the whole day working on a16-bar part for a pop CD and do an entire jazz record tomorrow. There are regional and national jingles in all conceivable styles as well as movie dates, TV shows, and countless other miscellaneous recording sessions.

While there is obviously a great amount of variety in the kind of music I'm called for, the fun comes when I can mix it up. At this level, all the musical bases are expected to be covered, both conceptually and instrumentally. For example, I can use a Fender Telecaster to play on a country-rock track and a Gibson ES-175 or a 335 to play straight-ahead jazz. But the creativity really starts to flow when I go against the traditional vein, like using a hollow-body jazz guitar on a heavy grunge song. For me, these are the kinds of situations that keep things interesting.

As with anything you do, you've got to keep it interesting. We start to lose our edges when things become too commonplace or too easy. Everybody gets burned out and fried from time to time, and we all need some distance to re-ignite the spark. I've hit upon the perfect remedy: When the studio scene wears me down, when I'm bankrupt of musical ideas, I hit the road with my band. Once again, variety. Nothing rejuvenates me more than playing live. It's the exact opposite musical experience from the highly critical, technically pristine, under-the-microscope performance one encounters between the headphones.

When I'm on the tour bus traveling across Denmark, hanging with the lads in my band, staring at the grass-covered farmhouses next to the icy blue sea and the green mountains against the blue and white springtime sky, it all seems like another world, so far away, in another time . . .

Hey, snap out of it! On the next page is a piece of music to pull you back to reality.

As you can see, it's in 5/4 time, with an accelerating tempo that goes from ♩=175 to 195. Musically, I'm not sure what kind of animal we have here . . . odd time, orchestral, heavy, progressive rock.

I played the top line with massive distortion. For me, it's always a challenge to make odd time signatures feel natural. The composer, Brian Bennett, had a track that felt great, so I relied on an old trick: As you play the notes, count out the beat until you can hear it, then stop counting and try to feel it. Since the 5/4 bar immediately following the 3/4 bar was a difficult transition for me, I wrote the beat numbers over the rests on beats 1 and 2. Over beat 3 I wrote "3+" to remind myself to come in on the "and" of 3. That got me back on the 5/4 track.

The acoustic part (on the lower staff) was a different pattern. The desired effect was more of a percussion part than a rhythm guitar part. Set your metronome to 100, count to five, and play this rhythm. Then try it at ♩=175 and imagine a gradual accelerando to 195. You'll wish you were on a tour bus daydreaming out the window on a beautiful spring morning. Believe it or not, I told the French guy that I enjoy this kind of thing. What was I thinking?

On the Road

Globetrotting with Supertramp

Those of you who follow this column each month might recall my earlier essay about making a new CD with the British rock group Supertramp. Upon completion of the album, I was asked to join the band. An offer like this generally strikes fear into the heart of a studio musician, because being out of town means missing gigs. But I have a serious need to perform in front of people, which goes against the grain of the typical session player. Besides, juggling three careers can't be much harder than balancing two, and unlike many tours I've turned down in the past 10 years, I like the band's music.

So, with the idea of taking a break from my group's three-sessions-a-day grind and infrequent four-guys-in-a-van touring schedule, I said yes to a world tour of 14 countries in five and a half months. The venues include 10,000- to 20,000-seat arenas in Europe (where the band is most popular and the record is number one) and 6,000- to 8,000-seat halls in the States. We're also playing the big three-day rock festivals in Europe with Kiss and Aerosmith, and these are 60,000-seat venues.

One of my biggest concerns about touring had to do with ear protection. The crowd noise in the big arenas is far more deafening than what's coming off the stage, and I want to be making records with these ears for a long time. So I was happy to learn, during the production rehearsals in London, that we'd be using an in-ear monitor system. These are those cyborg-like protrusions you may have seen sticking from the ears of rock stars, hairstyles permitting. The system requires having an ear doctor create a mold that fits a Walkman-like headphone speaker snugly into your ear. The speaker, in turn, plugs into a wireless radio belt-pack with a volume control.

During rehearsals, the monitor engineer gives your headset a little kick and snare, some hi-hat, overhead cymbals, and bass. Gradually, as you add the other instruments, you can construct your own little private CD mix, with your guitar and vocals featured prominently down the middle. What's wonderful is that all the updates are cumulative: Every little tweak to your mix makes it that much better from now on.

About six gigs into the tour I had it just right: A perfect vocal blend for singing harmonies and just the right amount of reverb on the guitar. Then I began to take things out of my mix and turn it down well below the fatigue level. I rely on the ambient sound of the main monitors to supply me with all but the essential things that need highlighting, like vocals, my guitar, and the ever-present Wurlitzer piano.

The advantages of the system are endless. First, the mains' engineer doesn't have that open-monitor racket flying all around the stage, so the sound is much cleaner and easier to mix. I'm using two Vox AC30s for my clean sound and a 50-watt Marshall slaved through a Marshall power amp for crunch, and in my ear monitors I hear them exactly as the microphone hears them. Gone are the days when you get a great sound onstage only to find out at the end of the night the mains' engineer couldn't make it work.

A second advantage is increased mobility. In the old days the monitor guy would need to follow you around the stage, putting your guitar and vocal into the wedges nearest you. With an in-ear system, your mix is consistent no matter where you go. Whether I stand by the drum riser or run down to the ego-ramp for solos, I can always hear myself perfectly.

Performers learn never to be dependent on the arenas for a good sound. Some of these venues (like the *palais des sport*s in France, bullrings in Spain, *sporthalles* in Germany, and hockey rinks in Canada) aren't exactly acoustically pleasing, but you can have a great gig nonetheless. And it makes for much shorter soundchecks because you don't need to change your monitor mix to suit the environment. In fact, on the festival gigs there is no soundcheck. They strike the support act's gear and you just walk out in front of 60,000 fans, pop in your monitors, and ream.

But the most important thing for me is the ear protection. There are no sudden spikes, thanks to a series of limiters in the signal path. With the volume control on my belt pack, I'm in control. I read that Jeff Beck wouldn't tour without an in-ear monitor system because his hearing can no longer take it. The fatigue you get from extreme volume is very real: You're beat the next day, and after a few nights in a row, you're really dragging. But on this tour I have much more energy and far fewer bad nights where I can't get anything happening musically.

Robin Fox, our monitor engineer, has taught me to react with the mains for my solos instead of turning up my mix. There are a few other subtle tricks that you learn with experience, but having been in the studio for the last 16 years, I adapt pretty quickly. And when the tour is over I won't have wasted a perfectly good pair of ears playing "The Logical Song" every night. You're bloody well right!

Rig Meltdown
When Bad Things Happen to Good Gear

The recording studio, with its expensive, high-pressure, deadline-oriented atmosphere, is the last place you want your gear to break down, but inevitably, this is where it will happen. No matter how simple or complex your rig, after subjecting it to daily transport, setup, teardown, and use, you'll eventually encounter that terrifying moment when you power up and hear nothing but the sound of your own quickening heartbeat.

To make matters worse, your cartage bill is costing your employers an additional $235 over and above your fee. They not only expect your rig to work; they expect it to get any sound they've ever heard a guitar make and to sound amazing doing it.

A knowledge of simplistic signal paths became useless in 1983 when rack gear, with remote, programmable effects-loop switching, came on the scene. The sound of the guitar changed, and rigs grew. I remember playing out of two 16-space racks with 100 memory presets (of which I used about four). It was stereo everything, with MIDI program changes gating my verbs and tapping my delays. Those were the days of major meltdowns.

I once showed up at a session for the movie *The Milagro Beanfield War* (which won composer Dave Grusin the Oscar for Best Original Score in 1988). My tube power amp blew a 6-amp fuse every time I tried to turn it on. After blowing all of my extra fuses, I bypassed the power amp, plugged my rack output into the effects return of another amp head, and panned everything mono. (Luckily, I had another amp; these were the days of preamp–power amp rigs.) After limping through the session (and volunteering for all the acoustic parts), I went straight from the studio to the repair shop.

These days, my rig is much more modular. The rack is considerably smaller, reflecting popular sonic trends, and it's not integral to the rig; if I don't need it for a particular sound, I don't have to use it. It's there for getting certain stereo sounds or getting a big sound quickly, but much of the time I'll use just amps and pedals. This eliminates many of the disasters, because I can always patch together something that works. If Marshall #1 needs tubes, I'll plug the pedalboard output into #2 or

#3. If there's no signal coming from the pedalboard, I carry a handful of extra pedals in my loose-gear trunk and even a few more in my car. There's no better insurance than having a good set of backup gear on hand.

Even so, while overdubbing on a number of sessions, I've had that certain special amp quit on me. These are the times when you're two-thirds of the way through the song and the amp starts to crackle or cut in and out. You can't change amps because your tone is dialed and the producer loves it. This is the time to have a good support team. On one such occasion, my guys at Andy Brauer Cartage company dropped everything, went to the store where I bought the amp, and borrowed another one. Then they brought the new one to the studio, patched it in, and took mine to my repair man. Since I'm a pretty big client (with 15 tube amps in constant need of maintenance), he had it up and running for my 9 a.m. session the next day. And the music store was kind enough to support their customer and their product with the loaner.

Every professional needs a backup team around town, because maintenance is everything. You need to establish supportive relationships so folks jump when you call and don't put you on the back burner. If you deal straight with people, pay your bills immediately, and convince them that your tone is the most important thing in life, that's a good start.

Sometimes, it's the little things that kill you, like an intermittent buzz or a hum you get only at one particular studio, or a nasty radio frequency interference (RFI) problem from a single pedal or effect. For this reason, my emergency kit includes spare pedals, an extra wah-wah in a dust-free Ziplock plastic bag (they're notorious session-stopping noisemakers), and a dozen spare quarter-inch cables. My cartage company also carries fuses for all my amps, with extra 6L6, EL34, and 12AX7 tubes on the truck. I also have extra tuners, batteries, strings, screwdrivers, Allen wrenches, power strips, speaker cables, female-to-female connectors, and the phone numbers of all the tech people I can count on.

All the major studios have techs and extremely well-stocked shops, and I've befriended those guys and enlisted their soldering chops on more than one occasion over the years. I've also learned a lot from hanging around repair guys while they're tweaking. The more I can know about the tools of my trade, the better my ability to think on my feet in an emergency.

But the best advice I can give is this: Be cool, calm, and collected. If all hell is breaking loose and there is a way to get up and running without making a scene, don't tell anybody, especially the composer or producer—they've got pressures of their own. The engineer is on your team, so confide in him about your technical problems, and try not to sweat profusely! Remember, it could be worse. I once saw a drummer do an entire four-hour session with his snare drum supported between his knees because he forgot his snare stand! He played the kick and hi-hat, too, and when he left the studio at the end of that day, he walked like John Wayne.

Scheduling

Practice . . . the Time Away

Some of the most frequently asked questions I've heard this year, especially while traveling with my band or on the Supertramp tour, relate to practicing. It seems like guitar players in every city are interested in two main areas of this subject: time and content. Under the heading of Time, there are two questions: How much do you practice? Where do you find the time? The Content heading involves dividing up the time into areas of concentration. In this month's column, I'll present what works for me on both fronts.

Where does a professional musician find the time to practice? I've always believed that playing one hour a day only maintains your chops. Like all musical activities, playing guitar is a physical endeavor requiring a certain amount of dexterity. Therefore, an hour a day is merely a maintenance program designed to keep us at our present level. I believe we really start to develop when we break through that one-hour barrier.

You already know whether you're a morning person or a night owl. Realizing this is important, because, unique to each individual, there are certain times of day when our brains work better. I'm completely useless after 11 p.m., so I practice in the morning. If I have a 10 a.m. session, I'm up early to fit in some time before the phone starts ringing and I have to start my day. Otherwise, if there's nothing on the books till the afternoon, the perfect day starts with me pouring a great big cup of coffee and sitting down to work on my music for a few hours.

A lot of my friends find it easier to work on music late into the evening. This is especially true of the non-pros and the serious players with daytime jobs. Often it's the only peaceful time in the house. The only danger is the relaxation factor. If you use the guitar to relax, that is, play things you know and to strum pretty chords to help you wind down after a hard day—it's all fine and good, but you won't learn anything. That's not practicing.

In the recording profession there is a lot of downtime. Often, a 1 p.m. session starts at 2 p.m. due to extended overdubs, equipment problems, or complicated setups. I try to use this valuable time to continue something I'm working on or to maintain my solo guitar repertoire. Once again, with a big cup of coffee and a quiet corner of the studio, a very productive hour goes by (while you're on the clock!).

The road is an entirely different story, however. I began a long European tour with—in addition to my two suitcases of clothes—a "groove trunk." This was an old amp-head case packed with a small Squier practice amp, a distortion pedal, a Boss reverb and delay pedal, music paper, a DAT machine and mic, and assorted cords, picks, and batteries. All this was delivered to my hotel room along with a Fender Tex-Mex Strat. But then I realized I'm hardly ever there! When traveling the great cities of the world, I would much rather experience the streets and the museums than sit in the hotel room with my guitar.

Then I understand that it's all about scheduling. We do a 5 p.m. soundcheck on every gig day, followed by a catered dinner at 6 p.m. Show time isn't until 8 p.m., so there are a couple hours of downtime right there. I have my guitar tech set up the little practice rig in a tuning room somewhere deep in the arena, and then I flog away for two hours a day. In Spain we played in four or five of the bullrings. Show time wasn't till 10 p.m., so I spent quite a few hours in the little room with the huge winch, the big drain on the floor, and the meat hooks on the walls!

Now let's talk about the Content heading . . . what to practice. I don't believe in dividing up the practice session into 15-minute segments of various subjects such as sight-reading and improvisation. If I'm working on a Chet Atkins piece, it might take two or three days to get it under my hands. Therefore, I'll just do it till I've got it and move on to something else that interests me, like an Albert King solo or a Sonny Landreth slide lick. I think practice time is much more valuable if you're fired up about it, not just drudging through a measured menu of subjects.

In various interviews I've talked about keeping a "lick book" or musical diary, which I've done for the last 19 years. This ongoing catalog of musical ideas becomes a very valuable practice tool, because when faced with an uninspired period of time, I can always reference back a few pages and see what I was into two weeks or three months ago. This often sparks an area of creativity that takes me to new places, especially with lines. And I have around 15 notebooks stretching back to 1978.

As I said earlier, I also like to expand and maintain my solo guitar repertoire. If you call yourself a guitar player, you should be able to play something unaccompanied on guitar, not just the riff from a Led Zeppelin song or an Eddie Van Halen solo (although you should know those things, too). Whether it's a classical piece, an original, a Jerry Reed tune, or an arrangement of a Beatles song, it's all part of being a guitar player. And it opens up another door to performing.

After improv and solo guitar, I try to touch on ear training in one abstract form or another. Listening while playing is an invaluable experience and probably the way most of us learned to play. Instead of transcribing entire solos (a practice I adhered to for years), I'll take the happening licks after determining the chord progression. Once a new lick is under my hands, I try to integrate it into my own lines until it bears little resemblance to the original. Ear training can be practiced away from the instrument as well (a subject I wrote about in my December '96 column).

As far as sight-reading goes, once you've learned to read music, the gigs will help keep it up. I consider it a privilege to possess this important skill, and I enjoy the extra speed at which I'm able to access transcriptions, my own chicken scratchings, and classical pieces. Occasionally on a Sunday morning, I'll read through the solo violin sonatas and partitas of J.S. Bach. I never stop being in awe of that perfect form of single-line writing. It often inspires melodies.

A great deal of my practice time is spent writing and developing my songs. Most of my songwriting ideas come while I'm practicing, or as a result of practicing. I find it important to get that original vibe on tape right away, in addition to writing it down. A good rule of thumb: When inspired, roll tape. But I always write it down as well, because I'm much more likely to flip through my notebook than to dig through a pile of tapes. One time, at a very famous guitar player's house, I spotted two huge cardboard boxes of cassettes in the corner of his studio. I asked him, "What's on those tapes?" He replied, "Song ideas." I wondered, "Do you ever listen to them or catalog them in any way?" and he replied, "Nope." So I became determined to store my musical ideas on a format that wouldn't waste my time. And plain old paper works best for me.

These practicing categories are a loose outline of my own practice regimen. As I said, I don't attempt to touch on each area every day. But when these things are on my mind and I'm aware of my strengths and deficiencies, I'm much more in tune with the instrument and I feel a lot more confident as a player.

Now I'd like to know what *you* practice.

Demo Love

Don't Try to Improve on Perfection

Anyone who does recording sessions on a regular basis has at one time or another encountered the phenomenon known as "demo love." It's that moment that occurs in the tracking or overdub process when the composer, producer, or artist realizes that what they really want is what's on their original demo. Sometimes it's because they've been listening to the demo for weeks and it's the only way they can hear the tune; other times it's an ego thing, something they played that they want duplicated exactly.

When asked to reproduce someone else's ideas and sounds, I always ask myself, "What is it about this performance that is so special? Is it the tone? The choice of notes? Does it have a special vibe that nails the essence of the tune?" Sometimes in a wave of confidence I'll address those issues with the producer in an effort to come up with something better. If it's the tone they like, I'll get that sound and then try to create something musically. Sometimes I'll go for the vibe and see if I can beat the demo. And sometimes, when I can't think of a damn thing to play, I'll just happily cop the demo and shut up.

Not long ago, I experienced a form of reverse demo love. A producer I'd never met called to ask me to play on an R & B record. My rig was delivered by my cartage guys, so I strolled in, met my employers, and proceeded to listen to the tune. As the engineer was putting up the faders, I heard some extremely funky guitar playing for about three seconds before he muted the track. When I inquired about it, the producer said it was what I was replacing, and he didn't want me to hear it for fear it would influence me in some way. I told him I should hear it just so I'd know what not to do. He explained that it was a 15-year-old kid from the ghetto who had played on the demo, a non-professional who had about three strings on his guitar and an amp that barely worked. I could tell they were embarrassed about the track, so I dropped it and proceeded to make a quick chart for myself.

In the pre-rap glory days of the TV show *Soul Train*, I used to sit on the couch every Saturday morning with an unplugged Gibson ES-335 and cop all the rhythm guitar parts, cataloging them for just such moments. Sitting in a pocket playing a funky part for three or four minutes is one of the most satisfying aspects of our gigs as rhythm-section players. So I dialed up a clean tone using the middle position on a 1960 Telecaster Custom through a '65 Fender Tremolux head and added a little compression at the engineer's request. I ran down a few verses to settle on a part and proceeded to "pave" a skank-style part, top to bottom. ("Skank" playing is when you play all six strings but only sound one or two notes at a time, muting the rest.) Once that was on tape and feeling good, I beefed up the choruses with a stereo harmony part over the continuing skanky rhythm. The guys in the booth seemed happy, so I started packing up the Tele.

After we listened to the track, I once again expressed interest in hearing the kid's original demo track. Seeing no harm (now that he had what he wanted on tape), the producer agreed. What came through the monitors next was some of the most homegrown, in the ditch, greasy, cold-blooded funk playing I've ever heard. It sounded like his action was about two inches off the neck and his amp was about three minutes from death. You needed a miner's helmet with a headlight to dig the depth of the groove he was laying down. It was quite possibly the only thing this kid could play, but he played it with the utmost conviction. It was very real for him, and the song was truly built around this groove, much like Stevie Wonder's "Superstition" seems to emanate from that famous clavinet riff.

I couldn't believe they wanted me to wipe out such a soulful part. I began to argue in favor of keeping the kid's part and losing mine. The producer wouldn't hear of it; he preferred my approach to the kid's primitive street playing, and that was that. It was truly a bizarre case of reverse demo love. For once, I loved the demo. I tried to convince him of the mistake he was making, and then a solution came to me: They could use his track and I would add to it, providing the "slick" element that they missed. They wanted the track to sound expensive, not so raw. It was very educational for me on a playing level as well as a psychological one.

I pulled out a Chandler Strat-style guitar with lipstick tube pickups. They have a lot of high-end sparkle and they cut through the midrange muck of a track with too many guys on it. Using a couple of delays, an Eventide Harmonizer and a t.c. electronic chorus, I created a shimmering sound that I could swell into, or use to sweep across the downbeats under the kid's steady skank part. The producer loved it and erased a few extraneous keyboard parts, which tightened and cleaned up the track.

Whoever this kid is . . . *he bad*. I never got his name, but he taught me a lot about playing funk. The groove was completely different with his part in. It felt much better. How many times can we say we've come up with something that strong? I especially enjoyed the challenge of complementing it with an alternate, interwoven guitar part. Days like that keep it interesting.

Live in London
Don't Fret the Live Stuff

For this Los Angeles–based studio musician, 1997 was very different from the usual grind. I did quite a bit of traveling, both with my band and with Supertramp, periodically popping back into town to work on a variety of sessions on my "days off." So besides being about the busiest year of my career, it was also one of the most musically fulfilling. For me, the live experience makes the whole studio discipline a welcome change, a chance to substitute the exacting skills of perfection with the "in the moment" mentality of nightly improvisation.

Recently, it all came together when we recorded a live Supertramp album at the Royal Albert Hall in London. We chose that venue because it's a small, 3,500-seat theater with great acoustics. Since the band hadn't played for five weeks, we began our five-night stand a day early for rehearsal. Most of the rehearsal time was spent sorting out the gear and getting all the little buzzes out. I spent quite a bit of time getting the distortion tone exactly right and making sure I could hear everything I needed to. This wasn't difficult, because the Albert Hall is like a living room compared to the 18,000-seat arenas we usually play. I had just come off a two-week tour with my band in Europe, playing 400-seater clubs, so my jet lag was over and my chops were up.

The plan was to warm up for two nights (Wednesday and Thursday) and record the last three. Logistically, it was a big project, requiring two 48-track Sony Digital machines and a 72-input board. For this, engineer Ken Allardyce (Green Day, Fleetwood Mac) rented the Manor Mobile recording truck and proceeded to fill up 71 of the available inputs with no problem!

To start with, there were 11 tracks of drums and 15 tracks of percussion. The electric bass took two inputs—one direct and a mic on one of the cabinets. Since seven of the eight band members sing, there were nine vocal mics, allowing for the different stations we mobile singers would work from. The two horn players operate from wireless mics right on their instruments, so there were six inputs for the various horns. Electronic keyboards took up four more, while the Hammond B-3 was allotted three inputs (Ken likes to mic a Leslie cab with one mic up and two down). The grand piano took two more, and the Wurlitzer piano, the band's trademark instrument, took a lowly single input.

I play electric guitar out of two Vox AC30s in stereo for my clean sound. For the distortion side of my rig, I like to play in mono out of Marshalls. Thus, the three mics on the electric guitar combine with the two direct input acoustics for a total of five guitar inputs.

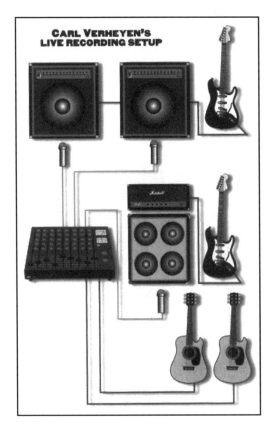

CARL VERHEYEN'S
LIVE RECORDING SETUP

There were some technical requirements, like six ambient mics for applause and one for a video feed, various samplers, and remote timbales. There was also an alternate guitar rig for the two-guitar harmony solos in "School" and "Crime of the Century," played by keyboardist/guitarist Mark Hart. The reason for the two 48-track machines was not to run them simultaneously, but to start one five minutes later than the other so we wouldn't run out of tape in the middle of a song. This also creates a slave copy of all but six minutes of music on each reel, eliminating the need to rent a studio and another machine later to make a safety copy. They simply did that at the end of each night.

Opening night went well. Everyone was fresh, and the Wednesday night crowd was rocking, especially for those polite Londoners. I used Thursday night's gig to correct a few monitor problems and tweak my amps a bit more, still warming up for the weekend recording. But when you've done a show 80 times, you begin to worry about your ability to make the next three your best, captured for posterity on a CD.

When Friday night came around, I felt prepared and ready, but as we began the set I felt very self-conscious about every note I played. I fretted (no pun intended) over the smallest and simplest parts, stuff I normally threw out night after night without thinking. As this was happening, I became very preoccupied with the performance: Was I moving around enough and did it look like I was having fun, or did I look completely stiff? With these two opposing thoughts raging away in my brain, it was amazing I could play at all!

Luckily, I spotted two friends in the audience and forgot all about the live recording. I just went for it like any other gig, till the end of the night when someone reminded me the tape was rolling. Friday night turned out to be my best night because I was distracted. For all the thousands of sessions I've done, even live-to-two-track recording, I was surprised at the psychological baggage that comes with performing and recording simultaneously. I learned an important lesson: Performing comes first and if that performance is sloppy and raggedy, then that's what it is. If the spirit is there, it will live and breathe a lot longer than a sterile and stiff rendering of the music. And that's what a live record is all about.

When Things Go Wrong

Expecting the Unexpected

Although we spend a lot of time and money each year on gear maintenance, there are those moments when an unavoidable failure happens on the session. Having alternate gear can help avoid a catastrophe. But there are those rare occasions when things break down or wear out right in the middle of a gig. In this column I will describe three disasters and how I walked away from them unscathed.

I arrived at Capitol Records' famous Studio A one morning for a tracking session. The first thing I noticed was that there were no other rhythm section guys, just a bunch of orchestral players. Sure enough, the music called for nylon-string guitar with the strings accompanying. There are usually two classical guitars in my guitar trunk, but one of them was at home on that fateful day. I opened the case of my old Ramirez A1 and found the D string was busted. Looking in the case, I found a full set of strings, but it was missing the 4th string. Even the emergency backup kit I keep in my car with strings, fuses, and extra tubes had no nylon strings. The session was about to start, so I had no choice but to play the first cue without a 4th string. Luckily, no one noticed me struggling.

It wasn't too bad, because the music could be fingered on the 5th and top three strings. But the next cue was very chordal. So as quickly as possible, I untied my A string from its post and retied it at the 4th-string post. Since my D string had broken at the bridge, it had just enough length to reach through the hole at the 5th-string post. I retied it at the bridge, passed it through the 5th string post, and carefully tuned it up while the conductor was counting off the next piece. It looked terrible but seemed to be holding. Just to be safe, I gave the studio runner a few bucks to run down to the music store and pick me up a few sets. And ever since then, if it's been a couple of weeks since I've played that guitar, I always check it. For some reason, nylon strings can break while they're sleeping.

Electronic gear like amps and effects are even more likely to fail, no matter how careful you are. One day I pulled up to a studio as my amp rack rolled right off the liftgate of the cartage truck and onto the ground. As the guys were gushing with apologies, I plugged it in and everything fired right up. But on another occasion, a session at CBS for composer/pianist Dave Grusin, I had a much bigger problem. At the time I was using a tube power amp in my rig. I was one of three guitarists on the date and the one hired specifically to play electric guitar. I fired up the rig 10 minutes before the downbeat, but my power amp blew a fuse. One by one, I went through an entire box of six 6.5 amp fuses as I tried to get the amp to turn on. When I realized it wasn't going to happen, I knew it was time to improvise.

At first I thought about trading charts with one of the other players, maybe getting the acoustic book instead. But I could tell the steel string stuff was very specific to Mitch Holder, as he'd already done a few previous sessions on this project. And the other guitarist was Angel Romero, a world-renowned classical artist. I wasn't about to touch his book! I had to stay on electric but I had no sound. . . .

I scrounged around the studio and found two reissue Fender Twins. I think one was Mitch's. I knew that the new ones have effect loops, so I borrowed this stereo pair, bypassed my power amp, and went straight from the mixer to the "power amp in" jacks on each amp. It took a minute to tweak the grounding and set the levels with the mixer, but I was up and running while they were still getting drum sounds. In my current setup, I would never have this problem because there are many amps I could use. But back in the '80s when everything was preamps and power amps, I can remember this happening a few times. It was at this time that I learned what a filter cap was and how it can go bad and blow fuses. Sometimes a malfunctioning piece of gear can kill your entire signal chain, so a good knowledge of your signal path is necessary to troubleshoot your rig while you're on the clock.

I think the most embarrassing problem I ever had occurred on a record project. I was overdubbing a solo on a pop-rock song, and it was just me, the producer, and the engineer in the control room. We had spent a long time choosing the perfect sound for the solo, and it was with a particular amp that I had recently purchased. My guitar was plugged straight into this amp with a long speaker line going out to a 4x12 cabinet. After about two hours of work, the brand-new amp started to intermittently cut out. Pretty soon, it just stopped working, and we were only about halfway through the song. I couldn't change amps because the character of the sound would be too different. And I didn't want to start over because we'd invested so much time into it already.

I told the producer to give me a half-hour break. The first thing I did was call the shop where I bought it. When I described my situation, they said they'd gladly bring another one to the studio, but I'd bought the last one in the store. So they called the manufacturer for me (who was out of state), and he located another one in a store in L.A. As a special favor to him, they brought me another one immediately, and it saved the day for me. I was indebted to everybody concerned because nobody blew me off. Sometimes it pays to do a lot of business at the same store.

I've had my wife and my cartage company bail me out on many occasions, too. Sometimes the one thing you need is the one thing you left at home. And if my baritone guitar goes into the shop for repairs, inevitably I'll get a call the next day for a baritone guitar. Under pressure, we all tend to think on our feet. The secret is to remain calm and collected. After all, it ain't brain surgery. It's only 12 little notes.

Working with Producers

Lessons in Diplomatic Relations

In the daily working life of recording musicians, we regularly encounter producers. By definition, a producer is someone in charge of the session that did not write the music (most often) but is responsible for representing the music properly on tape. Record producers are typically the liaison between the label and the artist, and the person ultimately responsible for turning in the project. It's a huge responsibility dealing with the music, getting good performances out of the players, overseeing the engineer, managing the budget, and coping with all the personalities involved. I'm always interested in how they work—especially because it often greatly affects how I work.

Some producers are very musical. When they're good musicians, especially good rhythm-section players, they seem to produce from the ground up, concentrating foremost on groove and feel. I enjoy working with this type because communication is much less abstract. You get something like "Carl, can you play the C minor figure on the 'and' of 3 and let it ring through the next bar?" instead of "Can it sound more yellow?" Then you have the non-musical but very organized type who knows how to hire the right band and to step out of the way and let it happen. Oftentimes, this type of producer is coming from an engineering background, and his forte may be getting sounds—sonic ideas instead of musical direction. Learn what to expect from each type of producer and know your boundaries. There are often politics involved, just as in any other workplace.

Years ago, I worked with a famous producer who slept on the couch through 90 percent of the tracking. His only contribution to the entire record was ordering dinner each night. Another time I showed up at a record date ready to rock, with all my gear delivered, and the producer let out a sigh of dismay when I introduced myself. Apparently he was expecting a different guitar player who was unavailable, and I was second-call. He told me this, and his rude manner shocked me. I said, "Yeah? Well, I just spent the whole day wiping and replacing that guy's tracks over at Record Plant Studio A." It wasn't true, but it put us on even ground. We got through the session that night, but he was abrupt, insulting, and showed so little respect for me that I never want to work for him again. I got a beautifully framed, triple-platinum record for that gig, but the experience was so lame that I keep it in the garage.

Once I did some overdubs for a famous producer who refused to let me look at the chart. He said it would corrupt my creativity and poison the track! The only drag was that it was a complicated, seven-minute opus with tempo and key changes, odd-time bars, and poly-chords like D/A♭—stuff you don't readily recognize. For all his experience, I'm not sure he knew how to get the best performance on tape, but I admired his energy.

Last week I got to work on a project with Eddie Kramer. As you probably know, he is probably the heaviest of all producer/engineers for us guitar players. Besides recording the Jimi Hendrix records and building Electric Lady Studios in New York City, he's recorded such classical monsters such as Julian Bream and John Williams. And Led Zeppelin. How are you gonna impress a guy like this? You mention a band like Traffic and he casually recalls, "Oh yeah, I recorded their first two records." It's a little unnerving, sitting across the glass from a guy who was *there* on many of your all-time favorite albums.

You might expect attitude delivered by the truckload with a guy like that, but I was surprised to find it didn't exist. You can instantly see why he's been so successful: He's in control. On this project, for a compilation CD of five different guitarists, I was the artist. He respectfully gave me the room and encouragement to develop my musical ideas while inspiring and suggesting new ones. The personalities clicked and the ideas and creativity began to flow between us right away. At times like this, working in the studio feels like the most fun you could ever have.

The first half of the session was all acoustic guitar. Before every overdub, Eddie would come out into the studio and listen to my part. (I was pleasantly surprised when he would then play it on the piano on his way back to the control room.) He put a very inspiring sound up in the headphones and the parts went down fairly easily. But the real thrill came during playback. All those years of experience were instantly recognizable. Not only did he have a *sound*, but also it was the right sound for the part I would play. Naturally, the same went for the electric guitar portion of the session. Eddie made it a comfortable environment to work in, both personally and sonically, and never lost momentum or control.

It's rare to find a producer with a serious engineering background who is also musically trained. More often, the musical ones rely heavily on their engineer, and the two work together as an inseparable pair. In situations like these, I'm all ears, because you can learn so much from these guys.

Enter each new working relationship openly and respectfully. You might learn a new mic technique or a sonic revaluation by *not* volunteering your favorite way of doing things. The same applies for music: There's always something to discover from even the most naive of musical minds (in fact, sometimes they're the hippest!). Give musical or engineering advice only when asked, because that's the producer's gig, not yours. Know your own self-worth and conduct yourself accordingly, but don't flaunt it. There's nothing worse than a player, engineer, or producer who spends the first half of the session telling you how cool he is, because . . . who cares? Their job, and ultimately your job, is to get the music on tape as the artist or composer hears it, and to see their musical vision fulfilled. Leave all ulterior motives in the lobby.

There will be a personality you don't click with, but that's just life. I've left the studio *hating* a producer only to hear the track later and really dig it. They can't all be Eddie Kramer, just like we can't all be Jimi Hendrix.

Radio IDs

Nightflying across the Atlantic

L ast month in this column, I talked about the wide variety of producers we encounter in our business. They range from the brilliant to the incompetent, and dealing with the different personalities is a large part of our daily workload. Sometimes you're exhausted at the end of a three-hour session, and you've only overdubbed rhythm guitar on one little three-minute tune! The people you work for can either make it impossible or make the time go by really fast, and when you understand this, you can often rise above a hard attitude by calmly letting your confidence show who's the expert.

Two weeks ago I was working for a good friend who's an excellent musician and a great producer: Mark Le Vang. Mark is a keyboard player, singer, composer, arranger, and producer who comes from a very solid Hollywood musical family. His dad, Neil, played guitar on the *Lawrence Welk Show* for years; he was also a studio musician who played on Frank Zappa's *Freak Out* record. Mark has done two European tours with my band and hundreds of sessions on keyboards and as a studio singer. Working for a producer, this is as good as it gets.

The occasion of our work together was a radio ID. Of the many types of recording sessions I've done—records, movies, television, jingles, etc.—the radio ID is one I've never talked about. Every time you listen to AM or FM radio you hear their little jingles between songs or before the weather or news broadcast. I work for a company that *cranks* out those little melodies for radio stations all over the world. Every two or three weeks they call me for a "broadcast package" for a station in Austin, Vienna, Florida, or Germany.

When I was last in London, I heard myself on Capital Radio and BBC 1, two of the big-three stations in England. So it was no surprise when I got this call. One of the composers was my buddy Mark, and the music was in every style imaginable.

The example I show here is in the style of *The Nightfly* album by Donald Fagen. Mark only had to mention this reference once and I was reaching for my Les Paul and dialing in a clean setting on a Fender Tremolux head. I remember asking Larry Carlton years ago what he used to get such a sweet tone on that record. He had recently acquired a vintage Les Paul and took that to the sessions. This stuck in my head, because it really shows the sweet, lyrical side of the Paul, an instrument usually associated with power chords and bone-crunching rock and roll.

In the first two bars I let the keyboards handle the rhythm stuff and played a few fills over the vocals. But in bars 3 and 4 the Rhodes piano plays a loose quote from "New Frontier," a track from *The Nightfly*. I jumped up to the top staff and doubled the piano in the octave written, which sounded in unison with the keys (playing *8vb* to concert pitch). The last two bars are an interesting reharmonization of the station's logo. The whole composing game is writing a catchy hook, singing the call letters of the station, and placing it at the end of a few bars of appropriate music. The melody and rhythmic syncopation remain the same, but the harmony changes for every ID we do. For a composition exercise, try harmonizing those last two bars a few other ways.

The only drag about these sessions is the length of the tunes. By the end of the day, you just want to play something that lasts for at least three minutes. It's a little hard to dig in and groove on a six-bar song.

Let Everything Ring

Lessons in Legato Playing

One of the downsides of the computer revolution in the music business is that powerful tool of every composer: the sampler. Samplers may have their place in contemporary music, but nowadays so many composers write their music on the computer. Therefore, they actually hear a guitar sample playing the guitar part before you get a chance to see it on paper. I have no problem with that, because the real thing always sounds so much better than the plastic, sampled version. But we run into problems when the composer (unless he or she plays the instrument) writes the impossible guitar part. One of the most common occurrences is when you are handed a page with stacks of notes or arpeggiated chords and told to "let everything ring."

No matter how big your reach is or how many open strings are available, you still run out of strings on a good many of the arpeggiated chords these keyboard-oriented composers come up with. Then it becomes a question of musicality. Since I can't make everything ring as instructed, the question becomes, "Which notes can I leave out to create the illusion that all notes are ringing?" The second question you need to answer is, "What would a guitar player do?"

I recently encountered this challenge on the entire score for a new movie. Craig Safan, an old friend from many years of working together on the TV show *Cheers* and the motion picture soundtracks from *Stand and Deliver* and *Mr. Wrong*, was the composer. Besides being a talented keyboard player, he can write some real "out" stuff, so it's always an ear-expanding treat to play his music. And the lack of pressure on his sessions makes me want to work even harder to get the results he's looking for.

On cue 5M3 I could play everything the synth-generated acoustic guitar sample could do up until bar 30. At this point I needed to be super creative to get the bulk of the chord to ring while playing the high G♯ in bar 31. At first glance you see a G♯m7 chord, an easy barre on the 4th fret (but note the enharmonic spelling of the 5th in the chord, D♯, as E♭ . . . stupid computer!).

The difficulty comes on beat 4, when the B♮ covers the G♯ you just played on the 1st string. And then there's the problem of that high G♯ way up on the 16th fret. Quietly fingering a few options, I solved this puzzle by the time the tape rolled by using artificial harmonics. Play the first five notes as you would a normal G♯m7 barre chord on the 4th fret. Then touch the 16th fret as you re-attack the 3rd and 1st strings. That gives you the B and high G♯ as harmonics while everything else rings.

The next chord in bar 32 can be finessed in a similar way: Use an artificial harmonic for the high note B on beat 4 by touching the 16th fret on your 3rd string as you re-attack that note. Finger everything else as an Eadd9 over G♯ on the 4th fret. The same goes for the next chord in bar 36. I let the B♭ in beat 4 ring while I sounded the artificial harmonic for B♮ in bar 37.

But in an effort to keep everything from sounding the same, I changed my approach in the next bar. You could probably figure out a dozen good-sounding ways to finger this chord, but I settled on a classical-sounding technique. I played the open A string followed by the E♮ on the 4th string, 2nd fret. Then I played the next two notes as open strings as well. But at this point, with my three open strings still ringing, I jumped up to the 11th fret on the 3rd string and slid the Fs up to the B on the 16th fret. This created a classical guitar–type sound, making the whole thing sound like a little guitar piece instead of a movie cue.

The next chord in bar 40 was easy. You can use the open E string, or finger the chord like a C♯m and stretch for the E♭ (once again an enharmonic computer error) with your little finger. Since I use that chord voicing all the time, that's what I did. I put the open E string on top of the very last chord in bar 42 and played the rest of the voicing in 1st position.

The accompaniment to the guitar was a small chamber group of strings, so these quiet, piano-like voicings were the perfect treatment. As I was leaving the studio, saxophonist Eric Marienthal was just arriving to play some soprano over the top of everything. The engineer was joking about how quickly the woodwind session would go down, compared to the six-hour guitar session. So I said, "Yeah, but he doesn't have to play any chords." Matter of fact, his instrument doesn't have any music with the instructions "Let everything ring"!

5M3

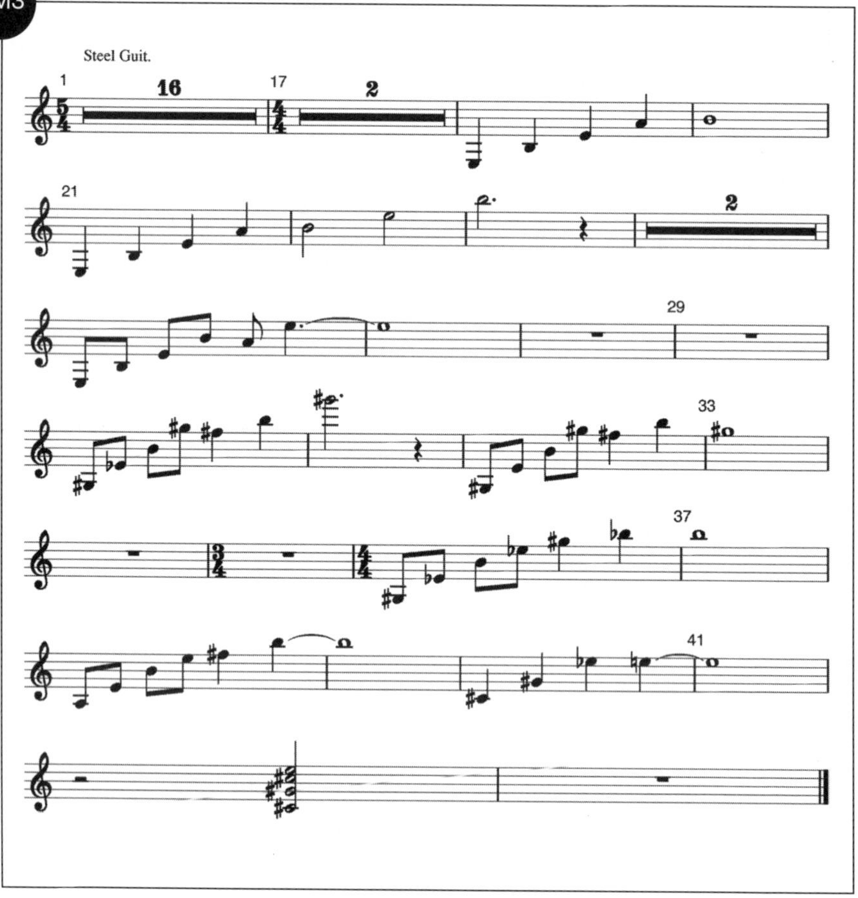

The Carlos Guy
Mentorship to the Extreme

Back in the days when I used to teach guitar lessons, I would occasionally encounter some real characters. Some of them were already good players and went on to become professional musicians with major league gigs; others didn't seem to have a clue. But the one constant factor in the successful players that I taught was a certain intangible quality: mental versatility. By this I mean a willingness to attempt the things that challenged them musically, a curiosity about sounds and the players that make them, and a healthy attitude about styles and musical genres. These are the things that make a versatile guitar player and ultimately a career in music.

One extreme case of the opposite school of thought was a 30-year-old man I remember as the "Carlos Guy." I don't know where he got my number but he had just moved to L.A. from Boston and he wanted a guitar lesson. He showed up in a complete tie-dyed outfit, head to toe. As he pulled out his Paul Reed Smith guitar I remarked, "Nice guitar." Then he replied in a thick Boston accent, "I do what *Cahlos* does. When Cahlos went to the Paul Reed Smith, I went to the Paul Reed Smith. When Cahlos went to the Mesa/Boogie, I went to the Mesa/Boogie. If Cahlos makes a change, I make a change."

As he began to play, I realized that his 15 years of experience playing the guitar was all concentrated into one musical goal: the emulation of his idol, Carlos Santana. I asked him if he played any acoustic guitar, if he knew any Hendrix tunes, if he listened to any classical music or had a favorite country artist. To all this he replied, "No, I only do what Cahlos does." His obsession with one style of music was so serious that he could not possibly be hired as a working musician.

A studio musician is coming from another entire galaxy of thought. But forget about the studio environment for now and think about your own "hire-ability." If someone called you tomorrow for a lead guitar position in a rock and roll band, I'm pretty sure most of you would take the gig (you and about a million other guitarists). But what makes you infinitely more hirable is the other things you can do, like play interesting rhythm parts or pedal-steel licks or rockabilly solos. Or play an hour of solo classical guitar repertoire. Or play through changes. Or sing. Each one of these skills opens another door for you to make a living.

In seminars, clinics, interviews, and probably even this column, I've answered the "how do I break in to the scene" question with my Pie Theory. I think of the music business on the players' level as a pie. If you can play heavy metal guitar, you get that one wedge of the pie . . . a pretty small piece. If you know a little rockabilly and can play some jazz standards, you're in for a bigger slice. And other skills and styles give you more and more opportunities for work. I'm always amazed when an average player is intolerant towards other genres of music. Unless you have a single-minded goal like the Carlos Guy, your own music will be so enriched when filtered through some bluegrass, country, classical, jazz, or blues study. Mental versatility means opening your window of acceptable listening.

Even though my own music is a crossbreed of blues-based rock, I have derived much inspiration and enjoyment from the following recordings:

1. *Tony Rice Plays and Sings Bluegrass* by guitarist Tony Rice
2. *The New Nashville Cats* by violinist Mark O'Connor
3. *Bach, The Lute Suites* by guitarist John Williams
4. *The Bridge* by saxophonist Sonny Rollins
5. *King of the Blues Guitar* by Albert King
6. *Standard Brands* by Chet Atkins and Lenny Breau

All of these albums are burning guitar records. They will require repeated listening and concentrated study, but the rewards are immeasurable. Just try to play some of this stuff, and you might have a whole new appreciation for an entire style of music that you previously rejected. Your own music will grow, as you become more versatile in the freelance world.

When my band goes on the road and I have a chance to talk to some of the players out there, my main piece of advice is: Learn everything you dig, and seek out the quality performances in other types of music that you may not particularly enjoy for the education. You don't have to be a musicologist to make a living playing guitar, but people hire you because they can't do it themselves. That makes you the expert. So it's important to know what you're talking about.

After telling the Carlos Guy all this stuff and ranting on and on about why he needs to listen to something other than Santana, I invited him to a live gig I was playing that night with a local band called Fingers. In addition to me on guitar, the players were Larry Steelman on keyboards, Ralph Humphrey on drums, and Alphonso Johnson on bass. Carlos Guy was delighted because Alphonso had been with Santana for many years and he was one step away from God. So he came to the gig and backstage after the show I asked him for his reaction to the intense set of music we had just played. "Didn't dig it," he said. "Ya didn't play any Cahlos."

There was no hope. The mental versatility just wasn't there.

Making Magic
Memorable Moments from the Recording of a
Commercial Jingle

Most of the truly memorable musical experiences in my life have been live gigs. Whether I played a solo guitar gig in a little 60-seat room, a 300-seat club with my band, or a 22,000-seat arena with Supertramp, I have wonderful memories of nights when it all came together—when I was actually happy with my playing and the audience responded accordingly. These memories are many, and at times they keep me going when the sound isn't right or my playing isn't up to speed.

But for some reason, the number of memorable recording sessions is far less. Take the audience out of the equation, slip on some headphones in an ugly, fluorescent-lit room, and the magic factor goes way down. That's not to say it isn't any fun, but as one cranks through ten or more dates a week, it's hard to remember what movie or record you played on Monday, much less two years ago. I have some nice memories of tracking dates on records I still enjoy hearing, but the day in, day out stuff slips right out of the mind in time for tomorrow's 10 a.m. downbeat.

The rare time when a recording session is a truly memorable musical experience for me is when the music is magical, the musicians and the people you work for are all first rate, the sound is perfect, etc. And—oddly enough—of all the gigs, this most recently came together and happened for me on a supermarket jingle!

I showed up at the cavernous Studio A at Oh Henry studios in North Hollywood carrying nothing but my Ramirez nylon-string guitar and a tuner. John Trivers and Liz Myers, an L.A.-based commercial, film score, and songwriting team, were the composers. I've learned to expect anything from these guys, from Arabic-tinged trance music to hard rock, Flamenco to soul music . . . and that's all in one week! John was the bass player in the Canadian rock band Prism before going on to work with Tina Turner and writing songs with Blue Oyster Cult. And that's him playing bass on "We Are the World." Liz is a classically trained pianist and holds a master's degree in composition. She also possesses a beautiful singing voice (I've got her on my new album) and has written 10 songs with Eddie Money. A more qualified writing team is pretty hard to find, and the musical variety that they present me with is always a welcome challenge.

The first thing I noticed was that Greg Bissonette, having pre-laid a drum track, was just leaving, and about 40 string players were arriving. I wondered why I didn't recognize any of the usual L.A. studio cellists and violinists—until I found out they were all members of the L.A. Philharmonic. I was playing with the Tall Dogs!

A real symphony orchestra is quite different from a rhythm section or even a group of studio string players. This point was driven home when Martin Chalifour, the concertmaster, stood up and said: "Perhaps we should take an A from our soloist." I looked around the room and then down at my music and quickly figured out . . . it was me! Having just arrived, I needed a moment to get my guitar in tune, and the musicians patiently treated me with silence. I'm not used to that kind of respect!

The music was challenging and exciting. The strings played an 8th-note figure while I laid out for the first 3 1/2 bars. My single-note entrance in bar 4 was in unison with the solo violin, but contrary to experience, I noticed I didn't have to back-phrase at all; we were immediately right together. This is rare, since bowed instruments generally speak late and rhythm-section rock guys like me always "prematurely articulate" when following a conductor. Maybe that's why I was digging the violas, cellos, basses and other violins playing some of the tightest 8th notes since those Billy Idol/Steve Stevens records! True pros, playing like a band.

Then in bar 10, it became my show. I needed to play the rest of the music as if it were a classical guitar piece with orchestral accompaniment: harmonized and fingered in a traditional solo-guitar setting with the melody soaring above the bass notes. Bar 12 gave me a clue as to what it should sound like. So I took off from there, filling in the harmonically "naked" bars (like 11 and 13) with bass notes and subtle counterpoint. The trick is to get it under your hands fast so as not to bore the orchestra, and make it sound like you've been playing the piece for years.

Some technical notes: I played the D♮ in bar 12 as an open string and let it ring until the downbeat of bar 13, where I played those notes plus an E in the bass. I went up to the 3rd of the D minor chord in the next bar to complete the rising bass-note phrase I'd started. Then I played an open D under the triplet, dropping down to the C for the downbeat of 15. Bar 16 worked as written, but 17 needed the bass note changed to a B♭ to make sense with the strings. I ended on the 18th bar with the chord as written, but I ditched the low F. The chord lays nicely on the 6th fret and made a nice finale to the piece. Although we rehearsed it, we didn't use the alternate ending. As a rule, I use open strings whenever possible on the nylon-string guitar. They sound great and provide a bit of classical ornamentation (to make you sound like you know what you're doing!).

Years ago, I did a few summertime outdoor pops concerts with Melissa Manchester around the U.S. I remember the rush of playing with the Cleveland, Detroit, or Chicago Symphony, but it was essentially rock and pop music, and I was on electric guitar. On this little 30-second supermarket jingle, I had that Segovia vibe going in a big way, with the cats that probably played with him! And I'll remember that for a long time.

Gear Maintenance
A Well-Kept Rig Can Save a Gig

In the course of a professional guitarist's daily workload, you encounter unpredictable situations. Playing live as a leader or sideman can require gear that is completely different from your recording rig. You try to make the right decisions and buy the appropriate gear needed to fill the task at hand. I've ended up with a whole lot of stuff: almost 40 guitars, 17 amps, and countless pedals and effects. And when I encounter a new or unusual situation, like a direct-to-disc record project or a live TV show, I can usually put together a working combination from my collection of equipment.

My live rig is a simple A/B amp setup with two clean amps and two amps for the distortion side. There is a small pedalboard, and the signal path is very straight ahead. It's a simple setup that gets only the sounds I want to hear, with nothing fancy: no high-tech chorus, no reverbs or delays, and no MIDI. I'd rather be challenged to get the sounds from my hands and a single guitar. I've learned over the years that for live playing, it's better to have two or three *great* sounds than ten good sounds.

But in the fast-paced world of studio work, guitarists are expected to draw from a broader pallet. Often a producer will reference a track on a particular CD during the session, and the guitar player will be expected to get that sound up fast. So the gear needs to be not only handy and fine-tuned, but also buzz-, rattle-, and hum-free.

The more stuff you use, the more time and money you'll spend on maintaining it. I've found that a few routine tweaks can keep my whole scene working smoothly. Here are the basics:

1) **The Guitars.** Although my cartage company offers a string-changing service, I prefer to do it myself. There's no substitute for the confidence that comes when I wind and stretch every string. And as with most Fender Stratocaster players, I have a personal routine I go through when restringing my guitar. By tweaking the claw and lubing the nut, I can make the old 6-screw floating bridge stay perfectly in tune. And when I keep my guitars intonated and properly adjusted on a regular basis, I never have to worry about pitch problems in the studio.

2) **The Cables.** As cords get lost, or run over and rendered useless by roadcase

wheels, they are usually replaced by something from the cartage crew's emergency kit or the studio's supply. Eventually, my cables become a hodgepodge of mismatched junk scavenged from all over town.

Recently, in the usual course of maintenance, I replaced all my guitar cords with high-quality DiMarzio cables. Everything sounds brighter and more alive. If you find yourself tangled up in a mess of old cables, try something new and you might be pleasantly surprised.

3) **The Pedalboard/Effects Rack.** My pedalboard is a hard-working little unit. I use it on just about every session or live gig I do. I take it on airplanes and leave it on funky stages between soundcheck and show time. Sometimes it stays overnight at a studio, when the cleanup crew comes in and vacuums around it. When not working, it lives in a small road case, but somehow it still gets really dirty. The whole thing needs a major cleaning every few months, but I never seem to get around to it—until something breaks.

Not too long ago, I had the entire thing rewired using the best wire available. This was another major sonic improvement that warrants repeating once every few years.

Rewiring every couple of years seems to be about right for my effects rack in the studio rig as well. High-end studio gear wasn't exactly designed for rolling on wheels and riding up and down on liftgates. The connections get loose and jiggle out of their sockets, new pieces are patched in and out, and the rat's nest grows. Approximately once every two years, I have my tech rip it all out and start over. I always hear a big difference.

4) **Amps.** Tube amps are hard to maintain. I'll work with my favorite old Plexi Marshalls for six months, and then they'll lose some of that richness, and sound a bit strident. At that point, it's time for new tubes and re-biasing. I'll take one of them in and have it tuned up, but sometimes one of my Fender heads then goes down. So I'm constantly picking up one and dropping off the other. I like to hang out with the tech and play through the amp when he's finishing up, to dial in the tones with *my* guitar. Everything is so variable and sensitive, particularly with the old Marshalls, so you have to keep on them. The same goes for Vox amps. Fender combo amps seem to run forever and then die hard. Some of the newer amps have that durability as well.

As far as day-to-day maintenance, I store and move my amps only in roadcases. I use the standby switch religiously, and I always check the ohm setting before firing them up. That's about all you can do; treat them right.

I also believe in the importance of surrounding yourself with a team of the best people available to work on your guitars and gear. These relationships will grow as you learn to trust your tech's ears, and that confidence will reduce stress on the gig.

Sometimes, this maintenance thing feels like a full-time job. Your days off are often filled with the responsibility of maintaining your gear, when you would rather be practicing and playing. But it's always worth it.

The Gunpowder Incident
The Difference Between the Studio and the Road

Just last week, while flying home from Europe, I had a few intense experiences. My band and I were returning from a month-long tour, exhausted from many nights of serious high-level playing and not much sleep. The band was Cliff Hugo on bass, Mark LeVang on keys, and Chad Wackerman on drums, and we were touring to support *Slingshot,* my new CD. The morning after our last gig in Amsterdam, we boarded a flight bound for California, with a layover in Washington, D.C. We had that "sleepy, glad to be going home" camaraderie as we left Holland.

On the first leg of the flight, I was using my laptop computer, and I accidentally ran the battery all the way down. Upon arriving at Customs in D.C., I was asked to turn on my computer. This is a routine bomb check the airlines always put you through, and for safety reasons I don't mind at all. The only problem was that I was out of battery power, and my AC cord was in my luggage, somewhere between planes. When a customs officer suspects something, you are escorted to another desk that has a big particle-analyzing computer, and the unidentifiable item is tested by wiping the sides with a special tissue. The tissue is then fed into the machine.

For some reason, my computer tested positive for explosives! Everyone (especially me) was visibly alarmed, so they tested again and again, each time with the same results. Supervisors were called in, and the battery and CD-ROM drive were taken out and tested individually, with the same result: explosives. And I was given the third-degree interrogation: "What's your line of work? What countries have you been to? Who's used this computer besides you?"

It was only when they asked if I had been around explosives in the last three weeks that I remembered the gig in East Germany. Instead of playing Berlin this time, we played near Dresden in a city called Bautzen. The concert hall was a converted World War II gunpowder factory, recently renovated from its dormant state into a beautiful 500-seat facility. The building had been derelict for 50 years, but the U.S. Customs explosives detector had found gunpowder in the parts-per-million dust residue on my computer! And this was only because I was storing it in the side pocket of my Stratocaster gig bag; the computer itself hadn't been anywhere near the concert hall!

I explained this to the suspicious officers and recommended they take a sample of dust from my guitar and gig bag. When they did, they found the particles to be consistent with the dust on the computer, and I was set free—but only after a multiple-page report was filled out with my passport number on it. It's very stressful to be detained while traveling, and especially to be denied entrance to your own country. My nerves were shot!

Safely back in L.A. the next day, I found myself struggling through jet lag on a jazz record date. I arrived at Mad Hatter Studios expecting to play some samba-style nylon string guitar on an acoustic piano–oriented record. I viewed it as a chance to break back into the studio scene gently after a month on the road. But much to my horror, composer Mark Gasbarro had written "the unison line from hell" for guitar and vibes. The tempo was ♩=200. Because of the 3/4 time signature, bars were flying by fast, and I hadn't read any music for a month.

On the road, you can get into a very artistic space. You work on your personal musical expression without having to deal with details like traffic and gear and scheduling. It's a chance to continually refine your improvising style, to attempt to achieve the perfect performance, night after night. You constantly strive for the highest level of playing and interaction with the band and the audience. The more shows you do, the more confident you become that this band is guaranteed to blow the people away.

So it was with this level of arrogance that I gazed upon bars 83 to 114. Barely recovered from the stress of yesterday's gunpowder incident, I was thrown back into the high-level pressure of the studio, on a date with players who could actually read eighth notes at 200 bpm! I worked up bars 83 through 89 in the 7th position, dropping to the 5th position for 90 through 99. From then on, I just grabbed the notes wherever I could. I played open strings in bar 105, jumped up to the 7th position in 108, and to the 10th position in 110. I found myself in the 12th position at bar 111, and I finished out the line in that general area.

At that tempo, fingering is everything. I tried to identify familiar licks that I play in the bebop idiom in hopes that they might already be under my hands—anything that would get it up to speed in a hurry. I also used every available lull in the session to work on the impending disastrous bars. For this reason, I was thrilled when the engineer had problems with a mic cable, and tracks 5 and 6 on the console weren't recording. Lucky for me, we ran out of time. Mark had a definite time limit at the studio that day, so it was "too bad, session over."

I was able to take the chart home for a few days. I have a lot of respect for Mark as a composer, so I really wanted to make it swing, and not just read the part. And this excerpt is only part of the story. There was more guitar and vibes unison line playing in the intro and the coda! I worked on it for a few days, refining the positioning to get maximum swing out of each phrase. Even so, when the day came to put it on tape, it wasn't memorized, just fingered and up to speed.

This isn't the hardest or the fastest thing I've ever encountered in the studio, but I will always think of it as a continuation of The Gunpowder Incident—two events that brought home a lot of perspective about the road and the studio, and how different they are.

Good Company
A Not-So-Obscure Tuning

Last weekend my band did a little California mini-tour opening for the Paul Rodgers Band. They put on a rockin' show, and we had a lot of fun with them. It was great hearing hit after hit from Paul's days with such bands as Free, Bad Company, and The Firm.

While playing at the Ventura Concert Theater, I had an interesting conversation with a fan who played guitar in a band that covered a few of my tunes. I was really flattered when he told me that he was the town's resident Verheyen expert!

He told me the biggest challenge was figuring out the obscure open tuning I used for the acoustic guitar part on "Carried West," a song on my latest CD, *Slingshot* (Provogue). He proudly announced that he finally cracked it after many weeks of listening, slowing the tape down, working and reworking the passages until he could play it right. The guy seemed so committed I hated to have to tell him I did it in standard tuning!

It's a simple Gm figure at the top followed by a bass line–driven progression for the verses. I wrote it on the classical guitar in the style of a little stand-alone etude that I could sing over, and when it repeated, I doubled it with acoustic piano. This seemed to enhance the dreamy, Frederic Chopin vibe.

I believe the acoustic guitar is a completely different instrument from the electric, and should be approached in an entirely different manner. On all my steel-string acoustics, I use at least a .011–.052 gauge set to get maximum tone and integrity from each note. Open tunings and capoes are tools of the trade that greatly enhance the capabilities of the instrument, and it's always good to have a high-strung (Nashville tuning) guitar, too. On this piece, however, my approach was from more of a classical guitar discipline.

On the four-bar intro of "Carried West" (Example 1) I played the first two and a half bars in the 1st position because the low B♭ in bar 2 is 1st fret, 5th string. Except for the bass notes, all the G and D notes are open strings, which may have confused the "open tuning" guy. And the second half of bar 3 is a series of slides on the 1st, 2nd and 5th strings with the open G string ringing. The harmonic in the last bar lies nicely on the 3rd string. I wrote the guitar part for the verses long after I had written the progression.

Once the melody and chord changes were in place, I sat down at the kitchen table and worked on the guitar part. I find that if I separate the composing from the guitar arranging, I'm able to come up with a stronger part and performance. And I always enjoy writing a piece of music that I can't quite play, something that I have to practice for a while to play fluidly. The verse is written out as a piano part so it could be doubled on the second verse. To get the right feeling, think piano. Imagine the sound you're making on the acoustic guitar is that dark, classical piano sound you hear on great Debussy and Chopin solo piano recordings. I use the pick and my 2nd and 3rd fingers on the right hand to roll the notes off, much like a pianist arpeggiates the chords.

The first bar of the verse (bar 5 of Example 2) stays in the 1st position, followed by a jump in bar 2 up to the 4th fret. Play the F/A in bar 2 in the 3rd position using the open A string. I stayed in the 1st position for beats 1 and 2 of the next bar, and then jumped up to the 6th and 8th frets for the E♭/B♭ and Cm7 chords. The D7sus-to-D7 bar is back down to the 1st position; sometimes the old "cowboy chords" work best!

In the 6th bar, I carried that philosophy a step further by playing my E♭ voicing as an open position C chord on the 6th fret. This gives you two Gs, one fretted and one open. I use the same voicing in the next bar with a B♭ on top followed by a descending bass line through the B♭/D, Cm7, and Cm/B♭ chords. (For this stuff use a Cm7 barre chord on the 3rd fret.) Bar 8 is a big, old A♭add2 chord on the 4th fret, and the last bar is an F7sus4 barre chord. The challenge is to make these last two bars sound as ringing and open as the rest of the music. Strong hands are required to hold down the A♭add2 chord, and especially to nail it in tempo. Years ago, when I first learned that chord, I practiced it all day until my hands were sore, but then I had it for life!

The song goes on to a big strumming chorus, a nasty Telecaster and snare drum breakdown section, a big slide guitar solo, and a three-chorus, mega-vocal ending. To tie it all together I ended with the acoustic guitar intro figure, thereby securing the "epic" status bestowed on it by drummer John Ferraro. He approached it like "Hotel California," and that brought it all together and gave each section a dynamic identity. I pre-laid all the acoustic guitars to a click so I could track with the rhythm section (on electric guitar), and make sure the band had the vibe. The only downside is that I would need three guitar players in the band to pull it off live. I wonder how the "open tuning" guy does it.

Soul on Soul

Getting Low-Tech 'n' Funky

Last night I got a frantic call from my old friend Rick Braun. He was under a serious time crunch, mixing his new CD for Atlantic Records called *South of Midnight*. As is often the case when a producer, artist, or engineer is midway through a mix, they "heard" something more, something else that was missing from the track. It was my good fortune to be the sound they were hearing, and I was available for a morning session on 12 hours' notice. Rick is a soulful trumpet player who's worked with people as diverse as Rod Stewart and Sade. He's on the new Bonnie Raitt album and we've worked together on projects for years, most notably his previous records like *Night Walk* and *Beat Street*. I dig him because he transcends that "happy jazz" vibe while still managing to get airplay on the adult contemporary stations. The tune was called "Soul on Soul," and he described it as a funky R & B ballad with a sweet vocal by Maysa Leak from the group Incognito. I wasn't familiar with her, but when I heard the track I recognized the voice. Rick gave me the task of "funky noodling," or urbanizing, the track. And listening down for the first time, I was inspired to keep it simple, not only musically but also in my choice of gear and my signal path. Instead of the usual percolating wah-wah part that you hear all the time on this kind of tune, I hooked up a Dunlop Rotovibe pedal and set the speed as slow as it would go.

Oftentimes, you get a vibe on the first run-through for either intro, verse, pre-chorus, chorus, or bridge, so a good engineer has tape rolling from the very jump. That way, if you get lucky with a certain part or feel, you won't forget it while experimenting with other approaches to the same section. I tried a different idea on each chorus, searching for the definitive part. But my first idea was the most intuitive, and engineer Steve Sykes had recorded everything. Having decided on the part, I pulled out the perfect guitar: a new Danelectro 56-U2. This super-inexpensive, lipstick-tube pickup reissue has that doinky sound in the middle position. It's a very unique voice through the Rotovibe into an old '65 Fender Princeton Reverb. For some reason, the slicker the track, the more I dig hearing and playing the low-tech stuff. It humanizes the often sterile sounds that synths and drum machines make, giving the track some character that those sampled sounds (and the whole "smooth jazz" idiom) often lack. I noticed Steve used a Shure 57 mic on a slight angle to the speaker, and ran it through a Neve 1273 mic pre into a Manley tube compressor.

The sound was natural and, with a bit of reverb from the Lexicon PCM 80, very inspiring. After printing all the choruses, we turned our attention to the verses. Sparse harmonics and a few R & B sliding 4ths were all that was needed, so I switched to my old '65 Strat. The Danelectro/Rotovibe combo was a sound you could easily overdo, and its quirky vibe was accentuated by the addition of a clean, unprocessed Strat sound. And a Stratocaster with a floating vibrato bridge is hard to beat for the pretty stuff. Once again we used the Princeton. I brought two black-face Princetons (a sweet little stereo recording rig), but we never felt the need for stereo. The simpler the better.

All that was left were the two bridges. I stayed with the Strat and found a little open string country-sounding part that worked over the descending changes: | D2 A/C♯ | Cmaj7 Esus4 |. With minimal gear, we ended up with three distinctly different sounds and textures in the song.

I hope this simple description helps to dispel the myth that studio musicians use racks full of gear to get the sounds you hear on records. I sure don't; I'm just as happy to find the sound in as natural a way as possible, eliminating everything that doesn't contribute to the tone from the signal path. It's almost always better when the engineer harmonizes or choruses your sound after you print it. Therefore you're better off printing the purest guitar sound you can, with an understanding that the engineer may effect it once you're gone. But at that point, he has an overview of the track that you may not hear during a guitar overdub session. You trust, and sometimes you're amazed, and sometimes you're burned. With these guys . . . I'm not worried!

Dealing with Rejection

Using the Experience to Improve Your Music

One of the biggest ironies about being a professional musician is the opposition of the business and the art. Forget about record companies, television, and radio—I'm talking about right down to the personal level. The sensitive, intuitive, and open characteristics of the artistic musician are often in direct conflict with the harsh, aggressive side of the music business. I've seen this inner battle chase a few very talented musicians right out of the rat race. They've all hung it up for the same reason: They just couldn't take the rejection any more.

We spend so many countless hours practicing, writing, and studying our craft. We put our hearts into something as microscopically small as a two-bar Fm lick at the end of a blues turnaround. We open ourselves to the sounds of our contemporaries and our heroes, listening for the slightest inflection of the hands. We put our souls into an extremely personalized rendering of a standard or a classical piece, polishing the arrangement for weeks or even months before playing it live. Those hours carry a large amount of baggage in the form of anticipation. Even musicians with the purest of artistic intentions must believe in the big payoff.

That's why rejection is so difficult for those of us with the artistic mentality. All of us have experienced it in one way or another—a rejected demo, a failed audition, an opportunity lost to a less-deserving player. All these situations force us to hit the streets again, to ply our trade elsewhere. Those musicians with the thickest skin bounce right back, channeling that loss and pain into a business sense of aggression with an "I'll show them!" attitude. The thinner-skinned players are more likely to be crushed or faced with an emotional setback, depending on the importance of the lost gig.

I've been dealing with rejection in one form or another for all of my 33 years of guitar playing. It starts when the big kids won't let you join their band because your amp is too tiny! It progresses into the club owner refusing to give your band a night because your music is not danceable enough. Eventually you find yourself rejected from a major tour because you have the wrong look or you're the wrong color. I've learned over the years to deal with these setbacks as rationally and maturely as possible. Experience is the best teacher.

Let's start with auditions. When auditioning for a major act, or even for a small club group, the reason you are there is simple: They need a guitar player. Whether or not you need a gig is unimportant. The most important thing is that they need you, and your attitude should reflect that. A needy, scratching, clawing, begging personality is a lot less likely to get hired than a confident, mature player. Go in there with an air of confidence: You would enjoy the gig, but you could also take it or leave it. This carries over to the final outcome. You are less likely to take it personally if you lose the gig to someone else. And remember that it isn't personal. There are so many factors determining the hiring of a band member, some as vague as "your vibe." If they can't hang with your vibe, forget them. You probably couldn't hang with theirs, either.

Many of us have tried shopping our demos or finished records to a label, with no success. Over the years I've heard all the reasons for rejection: It's not original enough, we already have a guitar player on the label, I don't hear a single, I don't know what category you fit into, etc. At this point, you really have to separate your artistic mentality from your business chops, because for the label it's not about your heartfelt art at all—it's strictly business. If they can't see the dollars and cents at the bottom line of your project, they won't sign you, no matter how good you are. And you can't take that personally. You have to believe in yourself and move on. Eventually, you'll find someone who can make it work. In the day-to-day business world outside of music, bids are rejected and sales are passed over every minute. The difference is that usually the salesmen are not emotionally attached to the product. Try to remember that to a label, it's product and not art.

In the studio scene, there are a lot of guitar players competing for the same gigs. Last week I was passed over on a two-day project because I wasn't black. This wasn't the first time it's happened to me, so I've learned to deal with it over the years. And if you turn the experience around, imagine how many times the guy who got hired has had to deal with racial discrimination because of some nearsighted producer's stereotypical ideas about musicians' abilities. We all get our turn. And the more you diligently work on your music, the more turns you'll get.

If a rejection is based on an honest lack of ability, like an inability to read music, or sonic deficiencies, channel that event into studying your music or working on your sounds. Along the way to becoming a professional musician, we get our butts kicked many times. It's the school of hard knocks. I learned to read music only after losing a handful of gigs that my contemporaries (friends who played bass and drums) were getting. Their careers were passing me by, and I couldn't let that happen.

At the time, I was devastated. My friends were starting to get some pretty good gigs, and I wasn't. But in retrospect, I see that it all happened for a reason. Not all kinds of rejection make you a better player, but believe it or not, the experience eventually pays off. Keep a good attitude. Good luck with your music.

Accept No Weaknesses

Recognizing–and Fixing–Gaps
in Your Musical Proficiency

When I sit down each month to write this column, I often try to reflect on how vast and diverse our readership is. Although we all share a common interest in the guitar, those of us fortunate enough to make our living playing the instrument do it in many different ways. Some play clubs, some do weddings and parties, and others play shows and musicals. Some of us get out on the road; some of us stay home and teach. Some spend their days between headphones, while others spend their nights between side fills.

Many of us, at one time or another, have done all of those things. Probably a lot of you have also moved up a career ladder, substituting quality work for the entry-level gigs with which we all started out. The main difference that I've come across in my travels is a philosophical one: The musicians I meet seem to have different goals as to how far they want to take their personal study of the instrument.

This is something to which I have a very hard time relating. Some people play guitar to meet girls. Others are musicians because they don't like to get up in the morning. I've even met a few who chose music school because it sounded easier than normal college!

Twenty years ago, I read a magazine interview with John McLaughlin, a personal hero of mine. It was one of those magical moments for me, because it put into print an ideal that I deeply felt and believed, and reading it at that age helped me to focus and had a profound impact on my life. When asked, "What made you return to the electric guitar?" he answered, "I'm always dominated by musical mandates inside me, and that's the whole reason for whatever changes I've gone through. I have to obey them, and my whole life is to serve my perfect-as-possible idealization of music and my role in it, in this world. And my ideals of music belong to the highest I can possibly conceptualize artistically and musically."

For me, this eloquently restated my own inner philosophy and challenge: A life studying music could not be taken lightly. There were to be no dark areas in my knowledge of the guitar, no weaknesses. I wanted to be able to play with the highest caliber musicians without apologizing for any musical deficiencies like sloppy chops, slow sight-reading, rhythmic incompetence, or inadequate sound. I wanted to be a "monster" like McLaughlin, Jimi Hendrix, Michael Brecker, or Vinnie Colaiuta. And every day I aspire to the lofty goals that inspiring musicians like these have instilled in me. After all, it's a life's work.

Where does one start, you might ask? The answer is simple: Practice your weaknesses. If you tend to rush or drag, or you occasionally drop a beat when playing with other players, you need to work on your time. This is easily done by working with a metronome or a drum machine every day. Eventually, you can set the metronome to beat on 2 and 4 so you have to feel where 1 is. If you are always the last one to get it on the initial run-through of a chart, you need to work on your reading. Find some treble clef books for practice. My initial investment into a sight-reading library included two flute books, two trumpet books, two saxophone books, two violin books, two clarinet books, and an assortment of reading study books for the guitar from places like Berklee in Boston. I tried to stay away from the exercises and concentrate on the melodic stuff like Bach. That way it was fun to practice, not boring.

Years ago, when I started putting together my own band, I realized a need to fluently write and read in the bass clef, too. So much of rock and roll is riff oriented, and so much harmony originates from the bass line. Unison lines phrased with the bass player are a staple of most rock bands, so the ability to communicate exactly what you want is an important writing tool. Without actually sitting down and studying it, I picked up the fundamentals of bass clef reading just by writing it all the time.

Then one day at a session, the composer asked if I could "jump down there and double the bass with a distortion sound." When suddenly confronted with 24 bars of 16th notes, I realized how slow my bass clef reading was. At that moment, I vowed to get a few bass clef reading books on my way home from the studio. I recognized a serious weakness, and decided to fix it. I couldn't tolerate this dark area in my musical proficiency.

The practice paid off, because these days I see bass clef all the time. Sometimes a composer is too rushed to copy out a guitar part, so he just prints a bass part and Xeroxes it for me. I'm expected to analyze the bass notes to determine the root of the chord, and whether or not it's minor or major, often on the fly. Other times an arrangement is enhanced by a guitar and bass unison figure, and it's not on the original guitar part. Sometimes you have to read from a double-staff piano part to fabricate a guitar part. (I believe the guitar should be written on two staves in concert pitch, like the piano, so I practice this once in a while.) Whatever the reason, it's good to have those chops at your disposal.

Musical knowledge, like your technique, should be constantly evolving. The minute we stand still, we drop backward, because music is moving forward. Every year I hear about new "monsters," dedicated players setting their sights on the highest musical proficiency their spirits will envision. The challenge to "get your act together before you step in here with me" is a healthy inspiration, and one that will take you many different places in your life. Accept no weaknesses in your playing, no dark areas in your musical knowledge.

The Chord Solo
Five Points to a Better Education

I practice a lot. It's a physical addiction. I enjoy pushing strings around, and the warm feeling in my hands after a vigorous couple of hours of intense playing. It's probably like a runner's addiction: They only feel good if they run; they get a natural high while they're doing it and feel funky when they miss a day. But I also enjoy it on an intellectual level. It's mentally stimulating to work out a harmony for a particular melodic passage, or come upon a fingering for something that was formerly impossible. And there is a subtle addiction going on sonically as well. After hearing so much bad music throughout the day, I have a need to replace this "unacceptable listening" with sounds that I make. After 33 years of playing the guitar every day, I'm hopelessly addicted to its timbre, the subtle changes from dark to bright, and the emotion a crying bend can evoke. I enjoy hearing simple chords resolve, dissonant chords clash, and the frenetic energy as sheets of scales and intervals stream by at breakneck speed. Sometimes I do it for hours just to hear it.

As I've said in earlier columns, I have never fragmented my practicing. Somehow I've managed to play everything without doing each one for 15 minutes a day. Instead of working on improvisation for 15 minutes, only to stop and practice sight-reading, I've always taken the organic approach: If the improv practice is inspiring, don't stop; do it until it becomes tired. Sometimes it is only after an hour or so that you begin to break new ground. Other days you'll feel like reading a Bach sonata or playing through a Coltrane tune. The key is to stay inspired so you put in the necessary time.

A good question I am often asked is, "What is the most important thing you can practice?" While I cannot point to any one musical direction or chop-building exercise, I do know of an invaluable skill that I use every day. That is the harmonic education I got from learning songs. Not just rock and pop tunes, but standards and jazz tunes as well. The many hours I spent learning tunes taught me more about music than any book or teacher I ever had.

My five-point method was simple: I would pick a song and learn the melody cold—in every register, all over the guitar. Next I would attempt to harmonize it with a straight-ahead chord-melody approach, using the "no-frills" changes in the fake book. With a little effort, this version would often serve as a solo guitar piece. Third, I would reharmonize the chord melody arrangement with an attempt to make it my own. This step would involve stripping down the harmony so I could use it in a band situation and not just as an unaccompanied solo guitar piece. Step four was the blowing section. I would work on playing a solo over the sometimes-difficult progression the changes laid out. And finally, step five was a cross-pollination of the melody, the chord solo, and the improv. I would attempt to play the melody while soloing over the changes and throwing in bits of the harmony here and there, putting it all together and making music out of it.

While this method generally applies to the jazz repertoire of standards, various versions of it can be applied to all songs. Individual steps in the process can be applied to the task at hand. In a recent session, I encountered the music you see here. Although there was an orchestral accompaniment, the effect was that of a solo steel-string acoustic piece. I slightly tweaked the melody to make the first two bars sound and play like Example 1 on the following page. Adding two bass notes per bar drove it along a bit more, and the open strings in bar two made it sound more guitaristic, almost like a classical piece (see Example 2).

I kept the bass line going throughout the song, so bars 3 through 8 should be pretty obvious. Example 3 is how I approached the D major section. I barred with my 1st finger in bar nine and again in 10. Bar 11 worked with just an open C chord. I made the downbeat of the 13th bar an A7 chord on the 5th fret, and used a series of descending major and minor 6ths to harmonize the melody. I kept it all on the 5th and 6th frets until the last eighth note in the bar, which I played on open strings, conveniently setting me up for the repeat.

Try putting this simple piece together for yourself before checking out my fingerings. See how well you can pull it off. I believe the many hours spent with the five-step song-learning method enabled me to get it up and running in about five minutes, after just a few readings. Having harmonized countless melodies in the past, it's now second nature to me, and I will often play a melody that way regardless of whether I'm asked to or not, just to get the vibe.

So you must immerse yourself in your practicing. Take all week to learn a tune. Make it your own. Learn it in other keys. Sometimes the simplest things you practice make you a mature and complete player.

Turning a Phrase

Fine-Tuning Your Articulation

This month was a very interesting time for me in the studios. I got called to work on a large variety of projects, and each day presented new challenges. Some of them really stretched my abilities, which is what keeps it interesting. The thing that really stretches my abilities, however, are scheduling. Trying to juggle the time requirements of a working road band and a career in the studios never gets any easier. Everything always happens when I'm gone!

I played on a lot of movies this month, which put me in large orchestral settings quite a bit. One movie I worked on was called *Three to Tango*, which involved not only Argentinean Tango but Mambo music as well. The nylon-string guitar was heavily featured in a big band setting. There were also the inevitable Brian Setzer rip-off tracks, which were very challenging—his stuff is not that easy to cop! I think he even plays on this movie, too.

I also did a nice pop-rock record with bassist Bob Glaub and drummer Jim Keltner. The difference between that session and a small group jazz record I did a few days later was monumental, not for stylistic reasons but for phrasing considerations. In fact, all of these gigs required slight phrasing adjustments. If you play in two different rock bands, chances are each will require a subtle fine-tuning of your articulation. If you're a good musician, you probably do it without thinking about it.

Some drummer/bassist combinations play way behind the beat, and require a feel that is equally "behind." Other rhythm sections play more "on top," much like Stewart Copeland and Sting did in the Police. There is no right way or wrong way to feel the pulse of music; each way has its own energy. But they both require a guitarist with a rhythmic feel who has an awareness of the placement of the downbeat.

However, these are only meter and tempo considerations. Phrasing is a term used to define the clear and meaningful rendition of music, comparable to an intelligent reading of poetry. When playing a melody, a continuous line is separated into its constituent phrases. One phrase ends and another begins. There is a sense of tension and resolution.

Options like whether to pick every note, hammer between adjacent notes, pull off on a few notes, use open strings or the 7th position are a matter of taste and personal choice—unless you're playing that melodic line with another musician. Two guitarists can easily work out the phrasing by sitting down with their instruments and synchronizing the slides, pull-offs, and bends. But in the studio a guitar player is often asked to play unison lines or harmony parts with an instrument that produces its sound in an entirely different manner than a pick or fingers striking strings, which results in dramatic changes in the way that instrument "speaks."

When playing with a string section, a guitar will always sound way ahead of the beat, especially when a conductor is involved. Just watch a symphony orchestra at work. They see the baton descend to the downbeat, move their bows, and a half a second later they produce a sound. By then a guitar is on the next staff! You've got to lay way back. Some brass instruments, like trombone and French horn, are a little late as well, but not trumpet. A trumpet is instant. Often it depends on the difficulty of the phrase and how cumbersome it lays on that instrument. You've probably even experienced this time discrepancy with synthesizers and sampled sounds in a rock band.

The musical example shown is from a TV show. At the time of this recording session, the show didn't have an airdate; it was being shot as a midseason replacement. Brad Fidel, who you may remember from the *Terminator* films, is

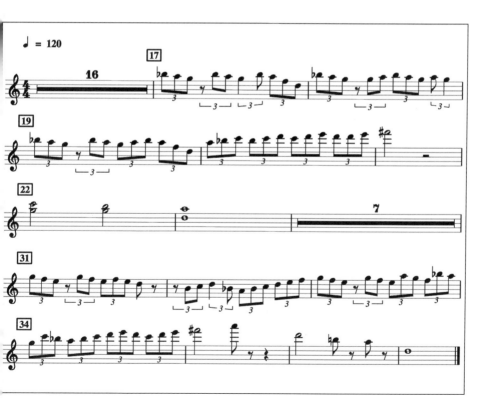

the show's composer when his busy schedule allows. Otherwise, his partner, Ross Levinson, handles the weekly writing chores. With Brad, I did a TV series some years ago called *Midnight Caller*, as well as many movies, including *True Lies*, *Striking Distance*, *Immediate Family*, and *Straight Talk*, and I consider him one of the best. There is always something fun and interesting to play on Brad's and Ross' sessions.

This particular example was interesting because the instrument with which I was playing this melody was a pennywhistle! That's got to be a first for me: electric rock guitar and pennywhistle. But because of the show's Irish stylistic flavor, the pairing seemed perfectly logical. The challenge was to make it musical.

Ross, who is a brilliant violinist as well as a composer, chose to write this piece in 4/4 time and use triplets. It could just as easily have been written in 12/8 time, but either way is fine; it almost looks the same. For dramatic reasons (it was probably a car chase), the tempo continuously speeds up, starting at ♩=120 and ending at ♩=128. This means there's a certain amount of rushing built in! And the pennywhistle plays instant downbeats—it's quite an agile instrument. With a big fat Les Paul tone, I felt like the guy with the cumbersome articulation. No longer will I cuss out those Johnny-come-lately string sections under my breath. I know what it feels like to be the slower-speaking instrument!

A little hint: Choosing the right position helps; in this case, it's the 10th for bars 17 through 23, and the 12th position from there on out. Set your metronome at 120 and give it a try. And just imagine a little pennywhistle guy sitting right next to you who is nailing it!

If It's a Gig, Take It

"Hawaiian Lap Steel? No Problem!"

Making a living in the music business is a day-to-day operation. Although most live bookings are scheduled a month or two in advance, studio work is often booked just a few days in advance. You start out each week with a blank calendar and end up working every day—unless, of course, your band has a tour booked; then you get called for three sessions a day (while you're gone)!

This tentative and irregular nature of the business drives many good players out. They get tired of the uncertainty of income and the lack of a steady paycheck. Those who can stick it out quickly learn this rule of thumb: Take everything. As you start out in the day-to-day practice of making a living in music, turning down work is not recommended. Eventually you can get picky about money, musical styles, hours, and players on the gig, but my advice is: If it's a gig, take it. This will undoubtedly put you in situations that are musically over your head, forcing you to learn on the job. But the fact is, most of my musical training has been while making a living with my guitar. Early on I subscribed to the "take everything" rule; once it's in your blood, you begin to say "yes" to all kinds of specialized work about which you know nothing. I've learned more about musical styles by being forced to play them in a pressure situation than by sitting down and transcribing the actual notes.

So the other day when composer John Frizzell called and asked me if I play Hawaiian lap steel guitar I unhesitatingly answered: "Sure." John is a happening composer with an impressive list of film credits that include *Alien Insurrection* and *Dante's Peak*. Not wishing to misinform him, I added that, although I don't own an actual lap steel guitar, I can get that sound on my slide guitar, and I have at least been to Hawaii a half dozen times. I also agreed to borrow a vintage Fender lap steel from my old friend and fellow guitarist Craig Copeland (a guy that could actually pull off this lap steel stuff for real).

I play slide guitar on a 1956 Supro Dual Tone with a big raunchy tone and a sawed-off bottleneck. I can play the blues and a little country in open E or open G tuning. The Supro gets two tones (you can't combine the two pickups): bright or warm. This old guitar distorts really well; the pickups are about three inches wide, yet they're single coil! (You can hear it on the solo in "Carried West" on my *Slingshot*

CD.) But the Hawaiians play absolutely clean and quite softly, from what I could tell. All the blues ornamentation like fret noise, undampened strings, and even vibrato, have no place in this music. Intonation must be perfect because without vibrato the pitch gets real sour in a hurry. Lucky for me, the bright neck pickup through a Fender Princeton absolutely clean sounded pretty close to a genuine lap steel.

So I set out to play this cue, and before long I realized that in order to articulate the double stops in the piece I would need to be in some kind of alternate tuning. Open E seemed to work because the song is in the key of A major, and the major thirds are sonically sweeter between the 3rd and 2nd strings. I played bars 1 and 3 on the 5th fret but bar 2 on the 3rd (beat 1), 10th (beat 2), and 12th (beats 3 and 4). The main thing was to make it sound as real as possible, so in this situation it's okay to add a few notes here and there, like the low D in bar 2. Bars 5 and 6 laid real well on the 5th, 6th, and 7th frets with very little moving around. I tried to avoid the high E string whenever possible, opting for the round tone of the B string.

Sight-reading slide guitar is almost impossible for me. You can't be looking at the music and looking at the frets at the same time. I'm not one of those monsters, like Bonnie Raitt or Sonny Landreth, who can nail the pitch without looking at the neck. So I needed to memorize this short little piece to see where it fell on the neck. If you don't play or own a separate slide guitar, tune your acoustic to an open E chord and try this satisfying little tune. It has a great vibe. We did a number of cues like this and it was a most enjoyable session. I overdubbed some *guitarino*, a tiny little guitar tuned a 4th higher for that Hawaiian ukulele sound. (I bought this $30 instrument in an antique store for my three-year-old son, but it sounded so good I snagged it for my acoustic trunk.)

One little interesting aside that made the date even more fun: The director was Mike Judge, creator of *Beavis and Butthead* and *King of the Hill*. He sat right next to me the entire session and, being a guitar player himself, he would say things like, "Wow, that was cool" after every lick I played. But when the guy opens his mouth, he's the voice of Butthead, so I couldn't stop laughing the whole gig. I kept thinking it was a guy doing Butthead, but it was really Butthead . . . it made for a hilarious afternoon. I'm glad I took the gig because now I can add the Hawaiian lap steel impersonation to my styles and the movie to my credits. In studio work, the number one rule of gig selection is: Take everything.

The standard notation represents the music exactly as it was handed to Carl. Carl played the melody up an octave (with the composer's approval). Which melody notes were to be slid together was left to Carl's discretion.

The Show Must Go On

The Importance of Having the Right Crew

Whether on the road or at home doing studio work, I always rely on key support people to make my gig possible. On the road, the band's crew and, more importantly, my guitar tech, are key. The person responsible for every last detail of my sound has a lot to deal with. From changing the strings to setting up and tearing down the stage gear to watching the show for disasters like amp failure or strings breaking, he's got his hands full. And on the smaller club tours (like those of my band in Europe), often that person is also road manager, bass tech, van driver, and merchandiser. These guys wear many hats!

When hiring a support crewmember, you can spot a good one immediately. Besides technical knowledge and physical ability, a good crewmember needs to have an incredible attitude and team spirit. I can best describe this vibe as a "show must go on" mentality: the unfearing attitude that, confronted with any disaster and against all odds, the show will happen. Robin Turnbull, my European road manager, is just such a soldier. From the North of England (where all good roadies come from), he is the most efficient, hardest-working road warrior I've ever met.

He can drive the van all day long, find the venue and the hotel in any city in Europe, and speak enough of the language in any country to instruct the local crew regarding the unloading and setup of the gear. Then during soundcheck, he can organize the dinner, set up the merchandising booth, and screen/schedule the various preshow interviews. During the show he remains just below stage right in case we need him, and after the show he'll supervise the load out, pack up and settle with the merchandising people, and collect the money from the promoter. Then he drives the band back to the hotel.

Back in his hotel room, there is the daily task of bookkeeping and tour accounting. All the receipts of the day need to be entered in the books as tour expenses, which come off the bottom line at the end of the trip. He finally gets to sleep long after us, but he's the first awake in order to rouse us sleepy musicians in time for breakfast, checkout, and the next drive. By comparison, playing the instruments an hour and a half a night is easy.

On big arena tours, it's the riggers who have it the hardest. Because they set up the lighting trusses above the stage, they're the first ones in and the last ones out. Often, they arrive at the venue at 7 a.m. and start wiring the lights. When the trusses are finally assembled and the entire rigging can be lifted, they still have a few hours of focusing and testing work to do. Only when the rig is flown can the stage crew get to work setting up the gear, and by then it is sometimes 3 p.m. And only when the show is over and the stage is completely cleared of guitars, amps, drums, keyboards, monitors, mics, and risers can they begin taking down the rigging. The rest of the crew is usually sound asleep by the time these guys drag it on to the bus. And they might get four hours of sleep—if they're lucky—before it's time to hit it again.

Back at home, when working the studios in Los Angeles, I delegate the responsibility of the transportation, storage, and setup of my gear to the Andy Brauer Cartage company. A crew of about 10 moves a handful of L.A.'s finest guitar players such as Dean Parks, Tim Pierce, Steve Lukather, Steve Ferris, and Michael Thompson. They also handle a few bass players including Nathan East, Neil Stubenhaus, Larry Klein, and Stu Hamm, and a few recording artists such as Joni Mitchell and John Fogerty. Besides storage and transportation of all my trunks of gear, they deal with the ever-changing nuances of my setup as it pertains to the day's session or live concert. Each member of the crew understands the signal path, and I'm always confident that my sound will be up and running by the scheduled downbeat time. They carry extra tubes, fuses, and cables in case a problem arises, and hundreds of feet of extra speaker cable for that occasional super-long run from the control room to a bathroom four doors down the hall.

One day last January, I got a last-minute call for a movie session on Super Bowl Sunday. I had already worked a few days on the film's score, and this was to be a pickup date for some additional guitar sweetening. I called in the day, time, and studio to the cartage company, but when I showed up at the studio, none of my gear was there! This was the first time in 10 years that I was stranded with nothing but a single guitar, and five minutes to go before the downbeat. And a high-level movie date at O'Henry Studio A costs somebody at least $600 an hour when you factor in engineer, second, studio time, contractor, etc.

I paged the crew but, because this was also the weekend of the L.A. NAMM Show, nobody returned my call right away. The composer was getting a bit stressed out, as he had budgeted the rest of the day for mixing immediately following the guitar session. Luckily I had the phone number of my old friend Stan Lamendola, head of trafficking at the cartage company. He was relaxing at home (probably awaiting kickoff time), but when my emergency came in he reacted in the true spirit of the "show must go on" mentality. He promised to make some calls to those nearest the warehouse, and if he didn't reach anyone, he'd do it all himself! Lucky for me, he reached a couple of guys and the gear was up and running only one hour late. And the error turned out to be a simple mistake: My session had been written down for the following Sunday.

I learned a few lessons: Always carry as many emergency pager and home numbers as possible. Always carry a small direct rig in the trunk of your car. And on Super Bowl Sunday, always double-check the schedule!

Trunkloads of Sound

Being Prepared with the Right Tools of the Trade for Any Occasion

Greetings from Paris, France. I've just arrived to do a couple of French TV shows with Supertramp in support of our new, live, double CD. There will be two days of rehearsal and three days of taping before flying back home. The events of the last five days leading up to this trip were quite hectic from a gear and logistics standpoint: It seems I never played the same guitar or rig twice.

Saturday my band had a concert in Ventura, California, about 70 miles north of L.A. But before the show I had to do a short acoustic set at a record store near the venue. For this I brought my Taylor 812-C, which has been outfitted with an EMF combination saddle and mic pickup system. This plugged right into the small PA with a stereo cable, allowing me to dial in a sound immediately and go! I only played for about 25 minutes, saving myself for the band performance that night. Appearing at these "in-store" gigs is more about meeting the fans and signing a few CDs than it is about performing, so they are pretty casual.

Next it was on to soundcheck. As you may remember in last month's column, I have nothing but respect for the crew that moves my gear. They were all set up when I got there; all I needed to do was plug in and turn on. For playing live I use two vintage Vox AC30s and two old Plexi Marshalls with a pair of 4x12 cabinets in an A/B system. There is a pedalboard and a small rack of delays and reverbs, too—it's a truckload.

The show went great, and afterward I stayed in a local hotel in order to get to an 8:30 a.m. start on a session in Santa Barbara (also north of L.A.) the next morning. For that session I used the Taylor acoustic, my '58 Strat, and a few pedals that I keep in the trunk of my car. The composer has a small Fender amp and we got a nice sound with a Shure SM 57 and his Lexicon 480 reverb.

Later on that same day it was back to L.A., where I did a nylon-string overdub on a movie called *The White River Kid*. Since there was no time to swing by the cartage warehouse and pick up my Ramirez, I used the electric/acoustic Takamine that I keep at home. This guitar records pretty well and we got the track in about two hours. I had never met the composer; I hope he doesn't think I'm perpetually exhausted! I was really wiped out that afternoon.

Monday morning I had a jingle for Post Select Cereals. No matter how tired or busy I am, I'll never say "no" to a national jingle. The money is just too great. Depending on how long they run the spot, that 45 minutes of work can make a musician as much as $2,000 a month for the next four years or longer (singers and writers get about four times that). This composer has a second-floor oceanfront recording studio that is not accessible to my huge recording rig. But he does have a direct rig already hardwired into his board, and he loves the sound I get through that stuff. It's a bit noisy, though, so I brought one of my DiMarzio-equipped newer Fender Strats with the Virtual Vintage pickups. It's pretty cool: You grab a cup of coffee, walk up the stairs, plug in, and start jamming as you watch the dolphins and sailboats go by!

We worked for about four hours on that stuff because there was a 60-, a 30-, and two 15-second spots to score. That, combined with a picky client, can make 120 seconds of music take all day. I got home in the late afternoon and crashed.

Next morning it was a blues guitar overdub on some independent Italian movie. Before the session I was played a tape over the phone for sounds. I was able to identify the music as an old Freddie King song called "Palace of the King"—a tune my high school–era rock band used to play! So I went by the warehouse where I keep my guitar trunks and got my 1965 Gibson ES-335 and my '69 Les Paul. (I have recently begun to enjoy the sound of my 335 again. The pickup covers had been in the case since I bought the instrument in 1976; I finally put them back on and now the guitar sounds sweeter to me.) But it was the Les Paul (with real PAFs) that got the fat and raunchy sound they wanted. I used the composer's Mesa/Boogie amp (I can't remember the model but it sounded pretty good). I put two rhythm parts down and then played a solo and I was out of there in an hour.

The next day I had a "triple header": three straight sessions. The first date was another jingle—some kind of Flintstones vitamin punk-ska-rap kinda thing! There were four trombones (which was pretty scary to hear first thing in the morning), four trumpets, bass, drums, and guitar. I showed up two minutes before the downbeat (not recommended). We all tracked together and finished in under an hour. I used my '69 Telecaster Thinline for that thin, offbeat, ska rhythm sound. I played through an old Fender Tremolux head that's part of my recording rig, and added a little slapback echo for a nice live sound.

Then I raced across town for a seven-hour radio ID session. This kind of gig requires recording those little radio station seven-second songs over which you hear the station logo. It's tedious work: You never get to play for more than seven seconds at a time! Once in awhile the band gets a killer groove going and they let us record a couple of minutes for a "traffic and weather bed." But most of the time it's short little five-bar cues.

Since it was a "smooth jazz" station from Dallas, I played a lot of hollowbody guitar. My '58 Gibson 175 and '59 Gretsch 6120 Chet Atkins were especially useful, although I did use my '65 Stratocaster and a Parker Fly for some of it. I also got a nice ethereal sound from one of those Parker Concert acoustic/electrics through my effects rack. I ended up changing guitars quite a bit to keep things interesting. We eventually recorded 32 separate pieces, so different guitar sounds became pretty important after a while. For this date, there were two keyboard players, bass, drums, and me. I got out of there at about 8 p.m., pretty fried.

But I had another gig: the final episode of the TV show *Turks*. Although I dig working for this particular composer and I had done all the other 11 shows in the series, I had tried to bail out of this gig for schedule reasons. When was I going to pack for Paris? But he would have no part of me bailing, so we started recording at 9 p.m. and finished at midnight. Because of the nature of the show this week, I only had my acoustic trunk delivered. I used my two old Gibson acoustics, a '51 J-50 and a '38 L-00. For the electric work I used my direct Lexicon recording rig, which consists of the Signature 284 amp and the MPX-G2 processor in a three-space soft rack.

Home at last after 11 hours of guitar playing, I packed my clothes for Thursday's flight. But in the morning I needed to do one last session before the trip. An old buddy of mine had a last-minute Acura jingle for me to play on, and guaranteed me out in less than an hour. So I took my old '61 Strat, which had been neglected all week, and plugged directly into the Line 6 Amp Farm system in his computer. We got a reasonable tone and did it quickly, in about 20 minutes. I got home as the limo was pulling up to take me to the airport.

When I arrived at the rehearsal studio in Paris, the instrument rental company provided me with a guitar tech, a very cool guy named Pascal. I needed a 12-string acoustic and he gave me a choice of three different guitars. I settled on a Takamine that sounded great. For electric I had requested a pair of AC30s, but the ones they had sounded kind of dull and in need of tubes. I used two reissue blackface Fender Twins for a nice stereo clean sound, which was fine for TV. The tracks we were taping didn't require a distortion sound, but I brought a few pedals for jamming, which is about all we did the entire two days of rehearsal! I brought a 1997 Tex-Mex Strat (I have one in maple and one in rosewood) in a gig bag, because they're easy to fly and sturdy enough to toss on the hotel room's bed.

I'm not sure if there is anything to be learned from this account of the last six days, except maybe this: Don't sell anything. After playing 18 different guitars this week (a few of which I've owned for 24 years), I would advise any serious student of the guitar not to sell anything that sounds good. You never know about sounds and logistics, or when you'll need a certain instrument. You can't own too many guitars!

Sight-reading for Sessions

Understanding Intervals Will Help You to
Transpose in Real Time

These past few weeks I've been doing some interesting sessions for a new animated series. The vibe is a '50s vision of the future where there is a gadget for everything and nothing works. On the very first gig, Chris Tyng, the composer, asked me what my favorite guitars were. I told him that my heart and soul are in Stratocasters, especially old ones, and that I can do anything on a Strat. To which he replied: "Don't bring any Strats. The show should sound like the dawn of electric guitar. Bad fuzz tones and squanky guitars like Silvertones, Gretsches, and Supros. Nauseating tremolos on twangy baritone guitar. Way too much treble on everything. Forget about tone."

Okay, a new challenge, I thought: I might have to go out and purchase a few of those "What were they thinking when they made these?" pedals; might have to put some tinfoil sleeves on the Rickenbacker 12-string for that pre-psychedelic buzzy anti-tone. Sounding bad takes some preparation.

The show has been taping with a 43-piece orchestra, and I've gotten some pretty weird looks from the string players: The approach I use to play the example 1M9 is similar to the way the string players read music. Sometimes it's not about the notes; it's about the intervals. Often, when they read a fast passage, they aren't thinking about playing each individual note; instead, they look at the relation of the notes on the staff to each other, and simply convert those distances to whole steps and half steps on the fingerboard. It's another level of sight-reading that goes beyond visualizing notes on the fretboard. At that point you're just looking at the distance between the dots on the staff, and making the necessary intervallic leap. This approach is especially good for transposition.

I can think of few things harder than real-time transposition. Horn players deal with it every day, and they use that interval relationship theory that I just described. In this musical example I was asked to play baritone guitar. This is an instrument that goes back to the mid '60s, when the Fender Bass Six came on the scene. Since then there have been many versions; the most popular one today is the Jerry Jones guitar. My bari, however, is a custom-made DeLap longneck that was a gift from Allan Holdsworth about eight years ago. I've experimented with it over the years and found that the optimum tuning is A, a 5th below the regular guitar tuning. Therefore my low E string is an A, and the open strings (low to high) become A, D, G, C, E, A.

Sight-reading on such a beast becomes worrisome, especially when 42 orchestral cats are waiting for you to figure out your part. So I approach the first note of bar one in its relationship to my bottom open string. The note is B with *8vb* (i.e., "down an octave") written below it, so this note sounds an octave lower than the B on the 5th string, 2nd fret. Since my bottom open string is an A, I simply play the B on the second fret of the 6th string, knowing that it's a whole step above A.

In bar 3, I don't have to stop and think about where E♭ is. I just play a minor 3rd above the C♮, my previous note. It's almost like being a kid again and not knowing where the notes are on the guitar! But if you understand intervals, you can transpose in real time. Bar 6 puts you to the test, however, because the downbeat B is on the 4th string, 4th fret—not where you'd expect it to be at all!

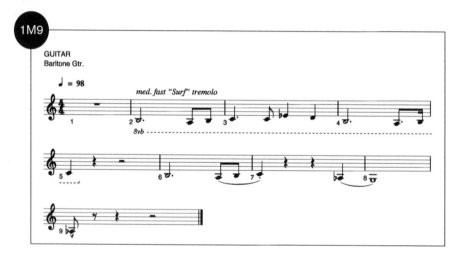

I wish you could hear the real genius of Chris the composer and his orchestrator Tim Simonec. The baritone melody on this cue begins a 5th below the bass notes, making for quite the overall sinister feeling of confusion. And the tremolo really messes with the bottom end. Bassist Chuck Demonico must hate me! It's a good thing the future didn't turn out like they thought it would in the '50s!

The Warm-up

Jumping Jacks on the Fretboard

've just returned from the First Annual *Guitar* Magazine Caribbean Cruise where I had the good fortune, along with fingerstyle wizard Doyle Dykes, of being a guest artist. *Guitar* Magazine editors Jon Chappell and Mike Levine were along as well, and I was amazed at how well they both played. And the international group of guitarists who signed up was made up of some of the friendliest, most appreciative people I've ever met. I would gladly turn down a week of studio work any time for seven days of playing guitars, eating, drinking, and sailing the Caribbean!

One of the many questions that were proposed to me through the week was, "Do you have any exercises for warming up?" At first I dismissed it with a brief, "No, I play all the time and I live in a perpetual state of being warmed up. It's my gig. And I don't believe in exercises." But then I started thinking about this past month and how work and life took me to some amazing places, not all of them conducive to practicing the guitar.

First there was the traumatic, life-altering fact that I moved this month; packing up a home of eight years is a huge undertaking. My music room was in boxes for a few weeks before and after the moving vans came, and packing took priority over practicing as the deadline approached. Next there was a quick trip to Madrid, Spain, to promote a new live Supertramp album. We did a photo session and a six-song television documentary, and I returned home the day before we were scheduled to move. As we began settling into our new house, the unpacking and setup of the new music room needed to be done just to make room for playing!

I was only in the new digs one week before it was off to Florida to embark on the *Guitar* Cruise. L.A. to Madrid takes about a day and a half each way when you factor in packing guitars and suitcases, airport drive time, international gate and customs wait time, layover time, etc. Live TV is especially high in the "hurry up and wait" category. Photo shoots? More of the same.

So there were days, even weeks, away from the routine. And I get pretty depressed when I pick up a guitar and it doesn't feel like the center of my life. I arrived in Tampa, Florida (the embarkment place for the ship), with a solo acoustic concert to perform to an audience of serious players in just a few days. At this point my chops were at an all-time low. So where does one begin to warm up after an extended period of dealing with the time-consuming business of life?

First of all, you must understand that the state of being "warmed up" is a physical state. That's why we play so much better in the second set, when the muscles in our hands have had a chance to stretch out. Sometimes I feel so good at that point that there is a euphoric feeling of invincibility: There is nothing I can't play, no idea I can't pull off. (I live for that!) Second, I believe there is no other way to achieve that feeling than by a lot of intense playing, and for me there are no exercises that come close.

But did you ever stop to think that there is another factor involved, that of being "in tune" with the instrument? Knowing where everything is on the neck, the physical distances between F♯ on the 1st string, 2nd fret and the C♯ on the 4th string, 11th fret. The distances with your picking hand between the 5th and 3rd string. The stretch your left hand makes when it fingers a B♭2 chord on the 1st fret and the same voicing for an F2 on the 8th. All these tolerances are subtle, but they make a huge difference in your accuracy and cleanliness when you've taken a few days off.

Somewhere down the road I learned a simple exercise to tune up the right and left hands and get the brain in tune with the instrument. Here's what you do:

1) Pick any note on the low E string and play it once. For this example let's make it a G on the 3rd fret.
2) Next, as quickly as you can, follow that note with a G on the 5th string. The position change has you jump up to the 10th fret.
3) Follow that with another G on the 4th string. You'll need to slide back down to the 5th fret.
4) Next play the G on the 3rd string. Avoiding open strings will necessitate a jump to the 12th fret.
5) Then play the G on the 2nd string; it's on the 8th fret.
6) Finally, play the G on the 1st string. You can get the one on the 3rd or the 15th fret, or play them both, as I often do.
7) Now that you've finished with G, start the whole thing over again using a different note, like B♭. Go through all 12 keys playing one pitch of the designated note on each string. Remember to do them as fast as you can.

Now here's where it gets interesting for all you pros out there. Do the exercise exactly as I described it, except without looking at the guitar. You should be able to play the six notes as 8th notes at ♩=84 when you are looking at the neck. Try to build up to that speed when you're not. As a variation, go from low to high strings and then back down.

There is no exercise I know of that gets me in tune with the instrument faster or more effectively. You are instantly alerted to scale length and right-hand string spacing as well. I believe that's half the battle, knowing instinctively where everything is. And all you guys who aren't quite sure of the notes on the fingerboard above the 5th fret will get over that problem in a hurry. So there's something here for all levels of development. Good luck and stay warmed up!

Exposure

Slow Bending on a Ballad

One of the more technically demanding things we do as guitarists is play lines in unison or harmony with another instrument. The guitar lends itself to certain phrasing characteristics, and each of us has an individual style as well. Nowhere is this more obvious than on a ballad, where the slow tempo seems to magnify every little turn and bend with which we ornament the line.

On a 12-hour country record date last week, I was confronted with just such a challenge as we approached the 11th hour. We had been tracking all day and, as is often the case, the other musicians left while I stuck around for a few guitar overdubs. One of the overdubs was the example you see in the music below: a simple five-note line over an ascending chord sequence.

Here is the original part with added embellishments.

There is nothing *technically* hard about it, but playing slow and milking those notes with the right *attitude* is the challenge. Notice the major 7th chord tone at the downbeat of bar 2. Without a passionate rock-attitude bend, this note just sits there and sounds completely sterile against the track. I used the vibrato bar on my Strat to scoop every note on the ascending line in bar 3, one of the many things I've learned from listening to Jeff Beck play ballads. And in bar 4, my right-hand phrasing went pick-hammer-pick-hammer-bend.

But there are many, many ways to phrase a line like this. The object is to find the way that is the most sincere and real for you. I used a fat distorted sound because the demo featured a slide guitar doing the line. Although they didn't want to duplicate the demo, they did want that sound and that attitude. This leads into the subject of bends.

Nowhere is your pitch more exposed than on rock ballad bending. With a slow tempo, it is mandatory not only that you reach the pitch but that the timing is right, too. By this I mean that *when* you reach the pitch is as important as reaching it. In bar 2, a long, slow bend into beat 1 sounds lazy and drunken. The bend needs to be strong and positive, reaching pitch with instant control and confidence. In a pressure situation where you are standing in the studio with a control room full of eyes looking out at you, and where, after every take, a half dozen mouths are jawing away without the talkback engaged, you need to summon that confidence. I try to remember who I am—the expert in the room on guitar playing; the authority on the subject of bending; the one they hired from a town full of good players to stylize this song.

With every take I try to dig in, to concentrate, to milk it and wring the notes out more passionately than on the previous take until it's the undeniably perfect, definitive performance. But along the way, producers will always throw in various roadblocks: It's their job.

One such detour might be the "change guitars" routine. Most producers are getting pretty guitar knowledgeable and tend to know the sonic difference between a Strat, a Tele, a Les Paul, and even a Gretsch 6120. As soon as I got the line nailed down and on tape, we switched to a Gibson ES-335 for additional "sonic girth." For me, this meant a major change of approach because there was no wang bar and, more subtly, the scale length of the neck changed. All my bends needed to be reconsidered for string tension and distance. I've done this a million times so it is pretty automatic by now, but the first run-through is usually quite a surprise. I always make sure to practice it silently a few times before cranking the amps up.

Another detour the producer might throw at you is: "phrase it exactly with the pedal steel guitar; we'll use both in perfect unison." This can be quite challenging, especially when the steel guitarist has gone home for the day and you're forced to phrase to his instrument's peculiar idiosyncrasies. All of a sudden the bending points are entirely different; you have to think like a country player instead of a rock player. I have checked out a lot of country records and pedal-steel licks, so I know the vibe and the "ornamentation" of the style. But in this instance, it took us further away from the original demo's David Lindley–style approach. Twenty minutes into the adventure, we abandoned that road for a different off-ramp.

And that off-ramp turned out to be the "octave up" detour. I was back on the Strat, had a slammin' version in the can, and they wanted to wipe it for an *8va* version. In my most diplomatic tone of voice I suggested we save the *8va* rendering of the melody for the fade out, where it is repeated many times. Luckily everyone agreed, and I played the first eight bars of the fade in its original register and then jumped up the octave for the second eight. As I neared the end of the second eight, I began to improvise, which led nicely into a solo . . . but that's a whole other subject!

Next month I'll spell out my string-bending exercise for getting in tune with tension, scale length, and working out all four fingers.

Bending Exercise
Six Bars for Four Fingers

Still a bit jet-lagged from a recent ten-hour-and-40-minute flight home from Amsterdam, I did a clinic and concert with my band for the National Summer Guitar Workshop people. We had just finished 18 shows in Germany, Holland, Switzerland, and Belgium, and I was basking in the pride of having a serious, kick-ass, super-tight trio and a show that blows people away by the second tune. There is nothing better for your chops than performing night after night in a challenging situation and spending your days in a tour bus being driven around with nothing to think about except how to play it better tonight. I live for that high level of musicianship.

We did a lot of festivals, including Guitarrenmesse at Rheinfelden with Robben Ford's band. At these events there was typically a band to open up for us, so we got to check out the local talent in places like Hamburg, Copenhagen, Stuttgart, and Berlin. Often, an opening act's guitarist would ask me for advice at the end of the show. Over the years, I've found that, in many cases, a player's weakness is in the ability to bend in tune, and in the feel of the vibrato. These seem to be the key elements of higher level playing that separate the men from the boys (and the women from the girls).

For vibrato, I always cite the example of Eric Clapton's solo in "Crossroads." The speed of the vibrato is so perfect that you could spend years trying to match that performance. I use it as a model, an ideal to reach for, every time I bend. And the intonation of the bending is so right on it makes me laugh at players who say they practice bending while looking at a tuner. Clapton never had a tuner in the Cream era—he used his ears.

Today the modern guitarist should be able to bend accurately and with a consistent feel with all four fingers. If you're playing an ascending line and you finish with your 4th finger, it should be able to bend up a half step, whole step, and sometimes even a minor 3rd with the same strength and consistency as your 3rd or 2nd finger. You should be able to finish any line you play with a bend, if that is what the music calls for. But getting all four fingers to bend as well as your 3rd finger is the trick.

Years ago, I devised a little bending exercise to introduce myself to a new string tension and scale length when I changed guitars mid-session. Because bending strings on a vibrato bar–equipped Strat feels so different from a hard-tail Les Paul, it is often important to tune up to those new tolerances in a hurry, especially when you're on the clock.

Requiring all four fingers to bend a whole step and a half step at least once, this melodic little six bars can be transposed to different positions for a more difficult (i.e., lower on the fretboard) or an easier (i.e., higher up the neck) left-hand workout. I've placed it in the middle of the fretboard on the 5th fret because that's where I always start. In bar 1 you have the benefit of playing the note and then bending to it, so your ear gets you started. Begin in the 5th position with your 4th finger and slide up to the 7th position midway through bar 3, where the tonality turns minor. Then alternately bend and slide down through the 6th, 4th, 3rd, and 2nd positions until you resolve back to C major.

Once the form is under your hands, you'll find it easy to play up a minor third in E♭ or down a whole step in B♭. But that's as low as you can go, because those 1st finger bends become impossible on the 1st fret. If you own more than one electric guitar, try it on your other instruments. You'll notice how different the string tension is even on two different Strats.

I've always found that practicing something with melodic content is easier than mechanical finger exercises. Take a few moments to memorize this little piece and you'll have it at your fingertips always. I think it will be worth it.

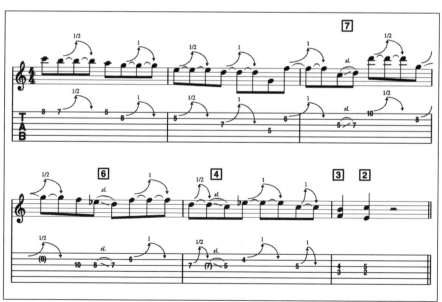

A six-bar melodic phrase that's good for practicing in-tune bends. The numerals in boxes above the music indicate position shifts.

Coda

When I was just beginning to make a living on the guitar and support myself, I took much inspiration from the drummers I knew. The drummers I worked with seemed to have it all together before the rest of us caught up. They could play all the styles, take any kind of gig, and, most importantly, read music. I realize now that there was no harmonic consideration in the various styles they had to learn and no pitches to the notes they had to read, but it still kick-started my learning efforts. I wanted no limitations on my abilities. I worked towards the day when I would be considered a pro, completely capable, a master of the guitar.

I still aspire to these ideals and hope to keep learning every day.